WESTONBIRT
Association News
2019

~ Bono malum superate ~

Westonbirt Association News 2019

Copyright © Westonbirt Association 2019
All rights reserved

Published in paperback and ebook by Hawkesbury Press 2019
Hawkesbury Upton, Gloucestershire, UK GL9 1AS
www.hawkesburypress.com

For further information about the Westonbirt Association,
please contact
Westonbirt School
Tetbury, Gloucestershire, UK, GL8 8QG
www.westonbirt.org

No parts of this publication may be reproduced, stored in a retrieval system, or transmitted in any form or by any means, electronic, mechanical, photocopying, recording, or otherwise, without the prior written permission of the copyright holder.

ISBN 978 1 911 223 44 3
Also available as an ebook

British Library Cataloguing in Publication Data
A CiP catalogue record for this book is available from the British Library

Contents

List of Officers	*1*
List of Vice-Presidents	*1*
List of Honorary Members	*2*
Editorial	*3*
President's Report	*5*
Headmistress's Report	*7*
Careers Events Supported by Association Members	*9*
Deaths Notified Since 2018	*11*
Sections News	*12*
Staff Section	*13*
Sections 1-87 (in reverse order)	*20*
Invitation to Association Members	*142*
How to Contact the Westonbirt Association	*142*
How to Order Copies of the Westonbirt Association News	*143*
Westonbirt Association Memorial Bursary Fund	*144*

(Section 77 Reunion photo on back cover
kindly supplied by Portia Ingram, Section Representative)

Westonbirt Association Officers 2019

EXECUTIVE COMMITTEE

President & Honorary Secretary Mrs Leigh Ralphs
Honorary Treasurer Mrs Karen Broomhead
News Finances and Distribution Mrs Jenny Webb
News Editor Mrs Bridget Bomford
Headmistress Mrs Natasha Dangerfield
Staff Representative Mrs Joy Bell

Co-opted Members
Mrs Serena Jones
Ms Karen Olsen
Mrs Mary Phillips
Mrs Debbie Young

Support Roles
Membership Assistant Mrs Jane Reid
PA to Headmistress Mrs Rhiannon Roche

GENERAL COMMITTEE

The Executive Committee and all the Section Representatives

2019 ANNUAL GENERAL MEETING

Saturday 16th May 2020

VICE PRESIDENTS
Mrs P Faust
Dr A Grocock
Mrs M Henderson
Mrs G Hylson-Smith
Ms Karen Olsen

HONORARY MEMBERS

Mr R Baggs
Miss V Byrom-Taylor
Miss D Challis
Mrs S Cole
Miss B D Cooper
Miss N O Davies
Mr P Dixon
Mrs Ann Dunn
Mrs D Elsdon
Mrs S English
Mrs L J Evans
Miss M Evett
Mrs M R Farley
Mrs J Hutchings
Mrs V A Innes
Mrs R J Kingston
Miss J Marr
Miss E M Miller
Miss P E Morris
Mrs H Nickols
Mrs H Owen
Mrs J Paginton
Miss O T Pasco
Mr D Philbey
Mrs M Phillips
Mrs H R Price
Mrs A M Reed
Mrs J Reid
Mrs A Rodber
Mrs D Thombs
Mrs C Tilley
Miss S Urquhart
Mrs M Walding
Miss K S Yates
Mrs D Young

Editorial

In last year's editorial **Debbie Young** maintained that no-one ever really leaves Westonbirt. I thought I'd finally left Westonbirt in December 2018, spending my final two weeks, as the very part-time archivist, at school sorting, displaying and storing all the fascinating archive materials. It's a good time here to say a big thank you to **Angela Potter** (Section 27) for inviting me to stay in her delightful guest wing whilst I carried out this work, and to the Association as a whole for financing all the storage boxes and other items required for the task.

Having safely displayed or tucked up all the archives, I thought I'd done with Westonbirt, but it was not to be! It was at this point that first **Rhiannon Roche** (PA to the Headmistress) and then Debbie herself told me that a new editor was required for the Association News, Debbie's career as an author having blossomed so well that she no longer had time to edit it. I said I'd think about it… then, in January, I found that I had somehow become the new editor, and here I am!

So, firstly lots of thanks: to Debbie for her years as editor and all her work in developing the Association News into a publication available through Amazon, thus making it more easily accessible to a wider audience as both a paperback and ebook; to **Karen Olsen** and **Serena Jones** (Sections 36 and 47 respectively) for their proof reading; to the Section Reps for chasing up their members and gathering all their news together, and to all you members out there who take the time, out of what I know are very busy schedules, to send in your news. You are all part of something very special.

I've found the whole editing process completely fascinating. One of the most wonderful things has been seeing how so many of you have kept in touch with each other for as long as seventy-five years – and without email, Facebook or any other technological tools! It's both encouraging and humbling to read the beautifully written news from ladies well into their eighties and even nineties. Not only this, but as I read, I'm recognising your names from the archives; from photographs of you, from artwork that appears in old House Books, and even from items of old school uniform from people like **Bridget Towel** (Section 30) (whose donations include lisle stockings that always amaze contemporary pupils) and **Angela Potter** (Section 27), whose swimming costume is still amazingly stretchy! At the other end of the scale, having been librarian and archivist at Westonbirt from 2007–2017, I'm finding it equally fascinating to catch up on the news of all of you that I knew in person; you are doing great things!

Finally, I ask for your forbearance for anything you think I should have done differently. I haven't had as much time as I would have liked to refine the editing as the bulk of the work began just as my mother had a heart attack, and travelling between Shropshire and Cornwall has been quite time-consuming, so again a big thank you to the proof readers and to Debbie for the final formatting and Amazon upload. I've tried very hard to limit any changes to your news and to keep the unique voice of all contributors, but after thirty years working in schools helping pupils refine their essays, please forgive me if I've changed something you would rather I had not!

Very best wishes to everyone for the approaching summer and beyond, and, providing this edition makes the grade, I hope to hear all your news again next year!

Bridget Bomford

President's Report

This time last year (May 2018) Westonbirt was celebrating its ninetieth birthday. A grand celebration evening with a Roaring Twenties theme took place on the Friday night, which was followed on the Saturday by the School's annual Picnic in the Park. The Association was invited to join in with the festivities and so we held our first Summer Reunion Day, rather than the traditional first Saturday in October. We had a marquee kindly provided by the School and **Serena Jones** invited a number of entrepreneurial alumni to showcase their business there. The display was very popular, and several parents wandered in and were fascinated to see what Westonbirt girls have gone on to achieve in their lives.

This change to a summer date proved so successful that we wrote to all the Section Reps asking them to indicate which date they preferred, May or October, and the overwhelming majority were in favour of May. So, we held it again in May this year and had a lovely day catching up with old friends and seeing how the School is operating in 2019. Most importantly, it remained dry and sunny! By holding it in May we are able to enjoy the buzzy atmosphere of the Picnic in the Park, with lots of families watching their children sing, followed by a live band for the remainder of the afternoon. A marquee had been set up with table and chairs for the Association and we were provided with picnic bags, delicious cakes made by some of **Mrs Joy Bell's** pupils, and plenty of Prosecco!

Our own HOWT (Holfords of Westonbirt Trust) guide **Angela Potter** took us on a tour which included the new archive rooms, brilliantly put together by **Bridget Bomford** (retired school archivist), with lots of displays of old school photographs and memorabilia. We rounded off the day with a short service of much-loved vespers in St Catherine's Church.

Next year will be the Association's turn to celebrate its own ninetieth birthday, which the School has kindly offered to host alongside the Picnic in the Park on around **Saturday, 16th May 2020**. Keep your diaries clear around this weekend if you would like to attend, and look out for further information from the School and Association nearer the day. It would be wonderful to get as many former pupils of the school as possible, back to Westonbirt for a massive reunion and sit-down lunch.

If you are also interested in returning to Westonbirt to talk to the pupils about your university experience, profession or business, please email **Mrs Jo Edwards**, Head of Westonbirt Business School, who has taken over from **Ann Dunn**.

Alumnae **Lucy Fenn** and **Tobi Arawole** came back to Westonbirt recently to talk to Years 10-13 about their careers and life at university, which staff and pupils valued enormously. Another opportunity to return to Westonbirt is for the **Celia Graham** Lacrosse Match, which this year takes place on **Saturday 7th September 2019** – last year's match was a great success (see the team photo on the Association's Facebook page). If anyone is interested in playing or supporting, please email **Rhiannon Roche** to book in for a team tea or contact **Steph Thorndyke** (Section 84) via the School.

The Association continues to support the Memorial Bursary, a fund set up in the late 1940s in memory of the five former Westonbirt pupils who lost their lives during the Second World War whilst members of the armed forces, civil defence or nursing services. Each year the Memorial Bursary is used to help fund the sixth form fees of one or more pupils who would otherwise not be able to stay on at Westonbirt or join for the sixth form. I personally find it a real privilege to be able to support outstanding students in this way and I would encourage anyone who is thinking of donating to the Memorial Bursary fund, or would like to bequeath a sum of money to it, not to hesitate, as you could be helping to change or shape a child's life. Further information about this can be found at the back of the magazine.

We have had a few changes on the Executive Committee team: **Bridget Bomford** has taken over from **Debbie Young** as Editor of the News Magazine. We are privileged to have her on board, and this is her first edition. I would like to thank **Debbie Young** for all that she did as Editor, helping to modernise the News and make it available to buy on Amazon. **Rhiannon Roche** is the Head's new PA and she also assists us with our administration and looks after the database. She has been helped this year by **Natia Jikia**, who has been our Study One Head of Association and will now be the new Section 88 Rep. We are trying to get to know the pupils whilst they are still at Westonbirt so that when they leave, they will know all about the Association already.

Once again, I finish with a plea for fresh volunteers to come forward to help the Association on the Executive Committee. We urgently need a Secretary – please email me if you would like to help or give back in this way: Lralphs@btinternet.com

My thanks again to all at Westonbirt who support the Association as well as those on the Executive who volunteer their time and all the Section Reps, without whose hard work we would not have this wonderful and unique News Magazine.

Leigh Ralphs

Headmistress's Report

As I reach the halfway point in this final term of the year and prepare to say goodbye to another group of leavers, I write to you with much pride about the ISI (Independent Schools Inspectorate) inspection which took place earlier this month and the developments that continue apace at Westonbirt. It was a pleasure to be able to address the AGM, although small in number, last weekend, and I hope now I can pass on some of the information shared.

In preparation for coeducation, the first phase of renovation has begun to transform the Old Gym and adjacent classrooms into the new Year 7 Hub, incorporating new Year 7 Tutor Rooms, and with at least one of the other rooms being used as a music classroom.

Alongside this will be a refurbishment of the nearest girls' toilets, and we will be converting the old maintenance sheds into new boys' toilets. The PE Department will eventually relocate to a more central position in the old paint sheds. New PE kit has been unveiled for the boys and subsequent conversations about changing the girls' playing shirts to match this very retro and reversible kit (the reverse design has a fabulous image of the school against a burgundy background) are underway!

Ensuring that we have the right spaces available for the children is important and therefore this summer will see the old bike shed area transformed into an outdoor space for Years 7 and 8 to enjoy, with areas, some under cover, to sit and climb, and outdoor table tennis tables for break time activity. Two new spaces in the old Holford House will be established as indoor areas and we will improve some quieter spaces for those who would seek it.

Exciting exchange programmes are still in progress and while we still have the girls' exchange with our Japanese partner school in Tokyo, we have also established an exchange with Lancaster Country Day School in Philadelphia. Service projects to India and Sierra Leone are now firmly in our calendar, with both trips secured in 2019 and 2020 respectively, and each focus on funds which support children in under-privileged areas, and their access to education.

And so, to our own education... having anticipated a visit for a few months now, we were pleased when the day of reckoning finally arrived. After three days and a significant trawl through all we do in and out of the classroom, we have been declared as an 'excellent' school for academic attainment and achievement and an 'excellent' school for pupils' personal development.

The inspectors were full of praise for the children and their attitudes to learning, their confidence and their care and support for each other. The comments regarding the children, the staff and the whole school community reflected the inspiring environment that we all know and care for so deeply.

To conclude, some information on The Holfords of Westonbirt Trust, who are about to start work on three key areas of the school, namely: the fixing and the refilling of the lake, refurbishment of the pavilions and the south side of the wall in the Italian Gardens and potentially a refurbishment of the Reading Room. The works of art which Lou Turnor curated for the school are proudly hanging in some of our state rooms and if you have not visited the archive areas of Holford, it really is worth the trip. Mary Henderson and I will shortly be joining forces to encourage some of you to visit, especially as the forthcoming year will mark ninety years of the Association, so if you are reading this – beware!

Mrs Natasha Dangerfield

Careers Events
Supported By Association Members

Over the last 12 months the Careers Department has seen some exciting changes. After saying a fond farewell to Mrs Ann Dunn at the end of the last academic year and thanking her for all her support and dedication over the years, we then started September 2018 with a new head of department, Mrs Jo Edwards.

The careers department started the year with a hugely successful careers fair, with over 40 companies attending. We had helicopters, displays and a wide variety of companies from all different industries. Years 10-13 attended and were inspired by the variety and possibilities open to them. We were also joined by Sir William Romney School who were able to bring along some of their students to benefit from the day.

Careers lessons are now taught specifically to years 10-13 with the aim of taking them on a journey of discover, thinking about the life they would like to lead when they are older and the path they may wish to take in order to get there. Years 10 and 11 created motivational posters that focused on their interests and gave them the opportunity to think about their future. To help them to do this a number of speakers came in to talk to the girls on their own personal journeys. Katie McDermott, founder of Not Dogs, and Tobi Arawole, a Westonbirt old girl, were some of the speakers who gave the girls an opportunity to hear how the decisions you make at school can influence your future, but at the same time showed them that endless possibilities are available, with the biggest message being to follow your heart and not be afraid of failure. Seizing all opportunities and working hard pays off in the end.

In January we had an extremely successful Inspiring Minds and Routes Ahead day. This event was organised by the Year 12 Business students as part of their coursework. The day consisted of an inspiring talk by Elizabeth McCullough from Goldsmiths University about critical thinking. Again, various different organisations and individuals spoke about the opportunities they have to offer and the career paths they took. Lucy Fenn spoke about her experience on an apprenticeship course which gave the girls a fantastic insight into other options apart from university. The girls were able to walk around the Routes Ahead fair talking to various universities, GAP year companies and apprenticeships. Many of the girls felt truly inspired and it gave them a lot clearer understanding of the courses they want to take after leaving school. It gave them the opportunity to ask specific questions whilst being able to network and gain contacts.

Careers is not just taught in lessons. Our comprehensive Skills for Life programme means that Years 7-10 also have the opportunity to think about the future.

Next year the Careers programme will be even more detailed, with another careers event due to take place on 20th September, with the aim of 60 companies attending and more local schools, and even more speakers coming in throughout the year to talk to the students about different career routes.

If you are interested in getting involved in any of these opportunities then do not hesitate to contact Jo Edwards on jedwards@westonbirt.org.

Jo Edwards
Head of Vocational Guidance

Deaths Notified Since 2018

Name	Section	Date of death
Rosalind Cooling (Bentley)	11	22 December 2018
Sue Yealland (Simpson)	13	12 August 2018
Patricia Hall (Dickinson)	14	July 2018
Ann Ratcliffe (Forsell)	16	9 February 2019
Josephine Smith (Pick)	19	1 February 2018
Miranda (Mandy) Fraser (Varcoe)	31	27 September 2017
Judith McGill	38	February 2019
Sarah Rehman	47	January 2019

SECTION NEWS

Thank You to Section Representatives
The Association is enormously grateful for the hard work and attention to detail shown each year by the Section Representatives, who volunteer to collect and collate the news from their former classmates. Modern technology makes this much easier than years ago, with many of even the most senior members sending in their news by email. Some members have also found social media, particularly Facebook and Twitter, useful for newsgathering.

Thank You to Section Members
We are always pleased to hear members' news, so if you're a regular respondent, thank you very much for continuing to keep us posted.
 If you've not sent in your own news for a while, please don't hold back. Even if you feel you have nothing to report, we still like to know that you are alive and well, and that we have the right contact details for you. We also love hearing reminiscences about your own time at Westonbirt.

Youngest Sections First
We're continuing the practice of starting with news from the most recent leavers. In the early, heady days of higher education and careers, keeping communication channels open with their *alma mater* may not be a top priority, so with the newest sections at the front they won't have too far to look to catch up on their Section's news, and we do appreciate even the briefest of reports!
 In all sections, we have listed members in alphabetical order by their current surname, to make it easier to find your friends.
 If reading any of their news makes you hanker after a nostalgic trip back to Westonbirt, we'd love to see you at our annual Association Day, and the school also welcomes visits by appointment all year round. To arrange to visit, or for any information regarding the Association, such as the current contact details for your Section Rep, please do not hesitate to contact **Mrs Rhiannon Roche, PA to the Headmistress, via her school email address, rroche@westonbirt.gloucs.sch.uk, or by telephoning her on 01666 880333**

Staff Section

Section Representative:
Mrs Mary Phillips

Mrs Joy Bell Hello there to fellow Association members, I hope this year has been kind to you. I am still at Westonbirt and enjoying teaching in such a lovely place and with such a supportive staff body. We are working hard to be ready to welcome boys into Year 7 in September and - watch this space - plans are afoot for a redevelopment of the food room! I am very excited for future generations.

Mrs Bridget Bomford I am, for my sins, the new editor of this fine publication! As of now, April 2019, it's been seventeen months since I left my position as librarian at Westonbirt, and three months since my very part-time role as archivist came to an end. Then, somehow, I've ended up editing the Association News.

My time since leaving in 2017 has been quite eventful. I left to help care for my ageing mum and mum-in-law, and to embark on mine and my husband's long wished-for move back to living as far out in the depths of the countryside as we could manage! Care of my mum is ongoing, we sadly lost Steve's mum in 2018.

Homestead-wise we were very lucky to find a half an acre of land, with planning permission, in a very rural part of Shropshire, down a winding lane and overlooking a water meadow and woods, beyond which is the canal. It teems with wildlife, which doesn't seem to mind us at all, strolling past or flying over us as we enjoy our coffee outside! We spent 15 months living in an aged static caravan, through one of the coldest and snowiest winters of recent times, and then through one of the hottest and sunniest of summers. We watched our new home being built, finding it difficult to believe we would actually live in it, but early in the New Year we did indeed leave the caravan and take up residence in our new home. Now the hard work really begins, as we tackle the job of developing our little patch of land into a wildflower meadow and wildlife haven.

Miss Valerie Byrom-Taylor The Ninetieth Birthday Garden Party at Westonbirt was a very happy occasion, then the following Saturday I enjoyed lunch at Chavenage where **Diana Challis** was celebrating a special birthday. The book for the ninetieth birthday is very interesting and beautifully illustrated. Just a pity that the Holford House photograph of 1971 was accompanied by the wrong names!

Miss Diana Challis It was lovely to see so many old girls and staff at the ninetieth birthday celebrations in May last year. What a splendid day too with Westonbirt looking at its best. I really cannot believe it but I celebrated my eightieth birthday in May last year! On a beautiful sunny day, I had a grand party with nearly eighty family and friends. I still keep very busy with activities in Tetbury, at the Arboretum and leading tours around Westonbirt House. It was fun leading one tour for a group of Old Girls who were celebrating forty years since they left Westonbirt; they told me that they never knew all that history whilst at school! It was a tour like none other!

Mrs Susan Cole I'm keeping well, and am still playing lots of golf, as well as doing my volunteering at Westonbirt Arboretum and stewarding in the church, singing with my choir, seeing friends and family, guiding at Westonbirt House, and going to the theatre. A big bonus this year has been the opening of an Arts Centre in Tetbury which is only a fifteen-minute walk from home, so I've been able to attend a number of exhibitions and films.

I've had some good holidays in excellent weather. In May I spent a week on the Gower peninsula with my family. We had lovely weather all week even though we had to wrap up warmly and wear hats. It is a really beautiful area. In June I was playing golf in East Scotland with **Mary Henderson, Sheila Urquhart** and **Sarah Nannestad (Nutter)**. We took all our wet weather gear with us, but it never saw the light of day, we were so lucky. July saw me on a tour of the WW1 battlefields, an excellent but very moving trip. I was in California and Arizona in September doing a tour of the 'Golden West'. The first week took me down memory lane when I visited many of the places I had seen in the early sixties when my father was British Liaison Officer at White Sand Missile Range in New Mexico. It was good to be there again, and to visit other places like San Diego, Yosemite and San Francisco.

I have just been appointed as Westonbirt Golf Lady Captain (for the second (and last!) time) so 2019 is going to be pretty busy for me. However, it hasn't stopped me from booking a golf week with **Mary, Sarah** and three other friends in Gran Canaria in May and I've just returned from a visit to Dubai.

Mrs Ann Dunn I've been prompted into writing this report because today is Friday 8th March 2019 and it is International Women's Day! So, of course, I thought of all the wonderful and inspirational current and former staff and pupils I've had the privilege and good fortune to meet over my long career at Westonbirt School. Retirement is sweet, and the stress has gone, but I do miss the people and the routine. However, now I have the freedom to play more golf, attend more fitness classes, meet up with more people and do whatever I please whenever I choose!

Mrs Dawn Elsdon (Mary Phillips says of Dawn '(She) is one of the loveliest and kindest people I know but she writes…')
    I am the most boring person! I really have nothing of any note to report. I am well and happy. Still helping to run Dursley Good Neighbours, with the help of my husband. I still belong to the WI and the book club. I meet up with three of my Westonbirt friends on a regular basis to swap news. Sorry I cannot be more exciting!

Mrs Dee Francis We are happily ensconced in the lovely Welsh town of Chepstow now after 15 years of living in Malmesbury. We have embraced life fully with classes at the local leisure centre and a History of Art course! I have also joined a choir, so life is very busy. We still find time for holidays and have just returned from New Zealand - a great place to spend January. Soon off to The Gower for a dog-walking holiday - I can certainly recommend retirement!

Mrs Mary Henderson Life continues to be busy in and out of Bath. A recent highlight was a trip to French-speaking Cameroon and Togo last November acting as interpreter for a group from Bath Abbey and Wycliffe Bible Translators. We visited the remote Banen community to see the positive effects of having the New Testament in their mother tongue, Tunen, and observed literacy classes in both countries. It was a privilege to have a job to do in these fascinating countries and to get to know the local people, not just as a tourist.
    I still work part-time for ACFEA, a company which organises music tours in this country and abroad. In March I am accompanying St Andrews University Chapel Choir on their concert tour of France, finishing in the cathedral in Aix-en-Provence, Bath's twin town. When I was a student I sang in this choir and in my third year spent six months studying in Aix so it is strange how the wheels of life turn full circle!
    I am enjoying playing golf in Bath and look forward to taking a group of lady golfers to Westonbirt at the end of May. **Sue Cole** and **Diana Challis** will be doing the tour of the school and Malcolm **Potter**, husband of **Angela Potter (Tracy)** husband, will show us round the gardens.

Last May sixteen friends and former colleagues made up a table at Westonbirt's ninetieth birthday celebration evening. We had a great time and it was wonderful to hear the good news about the future of the school. I spoke to the Chief Executive of Wishford Schools at the garden party the following day and was relieved to hear that he shared the values and appreciated the qualities which I believe we all love about the school. Now boys will have the opportunity to enjoy them too!

Mrs Jill Hutchings During the past year we have been pleased to attend our grandson's graduation ceremony at Leicester where he gained a 2.1 in Politics – a result we would never have dreamed possible as he pursued a very undistinguished career at school. At least he came good in the end, which might be an encouragement for any despairing parents or grandparents. He has now happily joined the working world. Our granddaughter is in her second year studying Civil Engineering at Brunel where she seems to be very happy, though we hear more about her exploits on the hockey pitch than anything about her course.

We chose the right year to spend our main holiday in the UK, since we had lovely weather for a trip to Cornwall and then to Pembrokeshire – an area we had not visited since 1964! For a final flourish we had a short visit to Bologna and Ravenna where we were able to marvel at the mosaics and enjoy some Italian cuisine. Next stop Antigua in April. Then we shall hope for a fine summer to enjoy gardening and local walks.

Mrs Helen Price Mary had this message from Helen 'Sorry, Mary. Life continues to pass pleasantly, but nothing new.' It is still good to hear from people, so thank you, Helen.

Mrs Gillian Hylson-Smith I am alive and well, still living in Bath and keeping busy, enjoying Pilates and the Abbey and seeing friends and family. Those of you who remember our Greek Orthodox monk son from Mount Athos will be glad that he has been promised leave of absence to attend my rather daunting birthday so that will be a great treat. Our love to all who knew us.

Mrs Mary Phillips This has been an unusual year for me. I was ambling along in retirement teaching once a week, doing granny duties for a day and a half, attending my fitness class, with the obligatory coffee to follow, and of course painting and drawing. In April I was able to do a stint at **Debbie Young's** Hawkesbury Upton Literary Festival, something I had not been able to do when I was teaching full time at Westonbirt. The summer was lovely, and Rob and I enjoyed a tour around France visiting our friends.

Then in September I got the call from Natasha to return to Westonbirt to cover for Mo Stockton who was absent for family reasons. Sadly, Mo was not able to return to school (she is fine) so I have continued and will still be here until July. I am loving the teaching, but it was a shock to the system after three years winding down to get back up to speed with the new A Level syllabus. Lots of things had also changed at school and there are many new faces, so it was a steep learning curve for me. While I have had to put several things on hold, I know I will be able to resume 'retirement' again in July. My family are all on good form and our sixth grandchild is due as I write this report. I have become a whizz at baking birthday cakes for them all and enjoy teaching them art, of course.

In January a number of Westonbirt staff were invited to attend **Philip Dixon's** play 'Nijinsky's Last Dance' in Bristol. 'Mr D', as many of you will remember him, was encouraged by former student **Alice Wordsworth** and so pushed on to complete the project he had been working on for thirty years. It was a brilliant show and Philip was delighted with the result.

There are many exciting things happening at Westonbirt and I have been reminded of the talented and committed staff who give so much to the school. I would like to tell you about a couple of them, starting with the music department, which is flourishing under the sparkling guidance of Mrs Nicola Atwell and you might be interested to note that Nicola has successfully started a Westonbirt Community choir.

Some of you will have done Duke of Edinburgh at school and this continues with groups going out and passing their Awards – to Brecon Beacons and Cheddar Gorge. This is under the guidance of Mrs Lexi Shea who also organises trips to India. The second one heading out in October with 17 Westonbirt girls who will be working at our partner school there. The girls are busy making blankets to take out to the Goodwill charity home and school in Tamil Nadu and would love to receive crocheted granny squares from you or indeed donations of double knitting wool. The girls are also planning to raise £5,100 which is the annual cost of education for a child at the Goodwill schools (Details, of the crochet squares, if you fancy making one, or of any of the things happening at school, are available at school reception). It really is inspiring to be in the midst of the buzz at school and to witness all the exciting things which are going on.

Mr John Sproule All our family are well. I'm enjoying retirement as is Ros who has taken up spinning and dyeing and is now a member of the Gloucestershire Guild of Spinners, Weavers and Dyers. We have a trip planned to the Outer Hebrides in June and are taking the opportunity to visit **Sheila Urquhart** and catch up on her news. Our children are all well, William is working for Nationwide, Tom is half way through his masters at Southampton University and Anna is travelling in South America having completed her masters at Sheffield last summer.

Mrs Diana Thombs It's hard to believe that I'm entering my eighties this year, though Tony is ahead of me there. I know I'm lucky in that the inevitable infirmities and illnesses of age are so far only minor ones. We abandoned the idea of moving to Nottinghamshire to be close to our two gorgeous grandsons aged four and one because that would mean leaving the friends and the home we have now known for fifty years. We see the family fairly frequently and otherwise the garden keeps us both busy while I'm involved with my local church, my book club and other activities. I meet former Westonbirt colleagues regularly and visit **Maggie Evett** most weeks at a local care home.

Miss Sheila Urquhart Although I live in the far North West of Scotland, I do seem to manage to catch up with a few Westonbirt people. In the summer **Mary Henderson, Sue Cole, Sarah Nutter** and I had a week of golf based in Dornoch and were very lucky with the weather. In November I went out to Taiwan and spent some time with **Teri Kao**, she is just as she was at Westonbirt but busier now that she has a little boy. In February I ventured south to the Westonbirt area and managed to catch up with lots of people; for those of you who remember Linda, (of Linda and Brian the taxi) she has not been too well, but she does remember all the students she and Brian took to airports, trains and Tesco. In between these trips I still enjoy being in Kinlochbervie and getting involved in village life.

Mrs Debbie Young I've had an enjoyable and busy year, publishing the fifth in my Sophie Sayers Village Mystery series of novels, writing the first in my new Staffroom at St Bride's series (about the staff of a girls' boarding school – all completely fictitious, of course!) and speaking at literature festivals and writing events all over the country. Working from home, I've continued to run the Author Advice Centre for the global non-profit group, the Alliance of Independent Authors (ALLi), and in April 2019 organised the fifth Hawkesbury Upton Literature Festival in my home village.

However, as I need to spend more time with my elderly parents and with my daughter as she tackles her GCSEs and gears up for A Levels, and because I have more new books planned than I can currently find time to write (including a new series set in a girls' boarding school!), I've decided to radically reduce my freelance work and volunteering and prioritise how I spend my time. I'm therefore leaving my ALLi job after six happy and fulfilling years, and standing down as editor of the Association News. I am very grateful to **Bridget Bomford** for taking on the editor's role, which she will do brilliantly. So, my day job will now be to write books – my ultimate plan when I left Westonbirt back in 2010! I feel very lucky to be in this position and am excited about the new opportunities it will bring me.

This year it's been pleasing to network with other Association members who are writing and publishing books. I was glad to be able to advise **Amiel Price** about her publishing project which has now reached fruition, and earlier this year I interviewed **Hannah Lynn (Phillips)** about her amazing achievement in winning the prestigious Kindle Storyteller Award, and published a feature celebrating her success on the ALLi blog.

I will still be ALLi's UK Ambassador and spokesman, so if any WBA members would like advice about any aspect of writing or self-publishing, please message me via my website, www.authordebbieyoung.com or catch me on Twitter at @DebbieYoungBN.

I will also be continuing to run the Hawkesbury Upton Literature Festival every April, a free event that gets bigger and better each year, so please do come along and join in the fun – find out more at the festival website, www.hulitfest.com.

I'll also still be running two local groups for writers, one in Bristol and the other in Cheltenham (which **Corinna Turner** joined last year!), co-presenting BBC Radio Gloucestershire's Book Club each month, and writing my monthly Young By Name column for the good old *Tetbury Advertiser*. So, I shan't be exactly idle – and I'm wondering how I've managed to fit in so much until now!

I keep in regular contact with former WB colleagues via Facebook and occasional get-togethers, including **Belinda Holley, Janice Malschuk** and **Charlotte Starkie (Rogers-Jones** when she was at WB), and of course all those on the WBA committee. I still maintain that no-one ever really leaves Westonbirt!

NEWS FROM SECTION MEMBERS

Section 87 (2018)
Section Representative:
Georgina Billingham

No news returned this year

Section 86 (2017)
Section Representative:
Thea Montanaro

Suzanna Battishall I am now in my second year at Reading doing Film and Theatre. I have been kept busy in the Film department which I am now majoring in. I have kept up with lacrosse and am now coaching at the uni.

Sonja Blickley I'm at Michigan Technological University studying Materials Science and Engineering. I'm involved in on-campus employment, and looking to get an internship involved in steel work this summer.

Alice Chubb I went to Budapest and Vienna in October which was great fun. I do philharmonic orchestra and we're going on tour in Prague soon. My team and university just won in varsity benchball too.

Cordie Cross I am now in my second year studying Photography at Solent University in Southampton. Certainly not taking for granted the beautiful trees that Westonbirt had, Southampton is very different! Just got back from an amazing photo trip to Paris. I'm enjoying being a part of the netball team this year and getting involved in the social side of the sport! Best wishes to everyone at Westonbirt.

Lottie Dickens I graduated from Oxford Media and Business School in July and I completed the Orchards Cookery course in January, in preparation for chalet cooking for the next ski season. In the meantime, I have applied for the Peligoni Club in Greece for the summer.

Camilla Edwards Since leaving school I have done a ski season in Flims, Switzerland, for five months, becoming a ski instructor. This was honestly the best time of my life, I would do it again in a heartbeat. I then went to Namibia for one month on a volunteering trip which was also incredible, and it felt great to be in such an amazing environment. I am currently at Oxford Media and Business School and hoping to move to London with friends and get a job once this course finishes in July.

CJ Egerton I'm doing amazingly as I'm currently at the University of Bath playing BUCS hockey and head of the Law Society committee whilst studying Psychology with an Education minor. Just booked a trip to the Maldives this summer and I'm going to Thailand for a month over Christmas. Welcomed my new baby sister recently and planning my future career in law! Good luck to all the old girls.

Isabelle Findlay I go to Oxford Brookes, and completed my Art Foundation last year. I now do events management here too, and I was working in a pub in Oxford, but recently gave notice as I needed a bit more spare time!

Kristie Fitzmaurice I backpacked Cuba for three weeks in September which was amazing and nice to have a break from technology too. I'm in my second year at Cardiff University doing Politics and Philosophy, which I am enjoying but joint honours can get complicated! I am enjoying being part of netball and band societies.

Isabelle Gent I am at Oxford Brookes University studying Music which is going really well, and I absolutely love it! I do lacrosse with **Molly Smith** which is great fun, we are both in the first team and have had an unbeaten season. I have been skiing a lot which is great, and I have enjoyed Brookes Entrepreneurs at university which is really good for societies and networking.

Lena Goglidze I am currently studying a degree in Psychology at Regents University and enjoying life in London.

Hunny Granger I'm at UWE in the first year of my Mental Health Nursing degree. I am really enjoying it so far and am currently in the middle of my first placement where I work in a rehabilitation ward. In the summer, I am climbing Mount Kenya for the charity Dig Deep; I climbed Kilimanjaro with them last year.

Lucy Holmes I remained at Westonbirt for a year as an assistant housemistress. I'm just working towards my NVQ Level 2 and working full-time in a nursery. I have also received a distinction in Grade 8 Speech and Drama.

Moyin Danielle Israel-Bolarinwa I'm studying Law with Philosophy at the University of Essex, which has a high workload but I'm really enjoying it at the moment. I really miss all my Westonbirt friends too!

Thea Montanaro I'm having the best time studying Geography at the University of Nottingham and I completed the East Midlands Tough Mudder with some of my close Geography friends last year. I have visited Amsterdam twice with **Kiera Segrave-Daly**. My family have also recently adopted a second rescue dog.

Alex Opgenoort I am currently at Aberystwyth University and in the kick boxing and clay pigeon societies. I work for the Stampede Stunt Company/Horse Combat and I am going to participate and represent the Netherlands at the World Championship in Digitovka 2019 which I am looking forward to.

Jessie Padday I am currently in my second year at Strode College doing an Extended Art Diploma. Having got a Distinction in my first year I applied to university and just received an unconditional offer from my first choice to study Costume Production and Associated Crafts at the Plymouth College of Art in September. I am also raising money for a charity called Dig Deep by doing a sponsored climb up Mount Kenya in July.

Emily Pearn Very much enjoying life at Oxford Brookes University studying International Hospitality Management. I am part of the public speaking society and enjoy attending talks at the Oxford Union. I will be going on placement next year, so will be in Bermuda for six months and then working in London for six months after that. It is so nice to have a handful of our year group in Oxford, just like the good times at Westonbirt.

Zaryna Pirverdi I'm currently in my second year at UCL doing the BA Education Studies course. My modules are mostly based on Psychology and I'm joining a few societies like the Economics and Finance and Business societies. I also work at software company Mealz as a marketing manager. I also visit tech-food events and business fairs where all food companies represent their brands. I dance Latino and do boxing, plus I've begun to travel a lot: France, Poland, Czech Republic and Italy so far.

Kiera Segrave-Daly After leaving school, I worked in the Old Bell Hotel in Malmesbury and on a vineyard in France to save up for travelling. I then went to India for a month and a half before meeting **Sharon** in Hong Kong. I then went on to South Asia and have visited Amsterdam with **Thea Montanaro** a couple of times. I am now studying English Literature and Art History at Leeds and enjoying continuing to play lacrosse.

Hannah Segrue I am currently at the Royal Agricultural University (RAU) doing Food Production and Supply Management which is interesting. I have already made friends for life and am off to Florida in the summer to go to Disney.

Sharon Yu I have really enjoyed everything Brighton has to offer as a city and often to go gigs. I am studying Geography at Brighton University and it is going well.

Section 85 (2016)
Section Representative:
Charlotte Price

Sophia Ashe Did my first British Universities and Colleges' archery competition in February and the last few clay shooting competitions are coming up. Dissertation hand-in needed and after university I am hoping to do farming work around the world, starting with a harvest in Australia from October and cattle ranching in America the following Easter. Considering a Masters in Rural Law after taking some time out but this is still under debate!

Emily Brooks I'm currently writing my dissertation/research project for my intercalated year and will hopefully be graduating with a Genomic Medicine Degree in July. I am then rejoining the medical course in September and will be doing a mixture of lectures and hospital placement at Southmead Hospital in Bristol and Weston-super-Mare General Hospital throughout the year. I am still playing lacrosse but will be handing over my first team captaincy at the end of this season! I'm hoping to try and find some time to travel this summer, and train for the Bath Half Marathon next year, wish me luck!

Katherine Edwards I'm graduating with a Geography degree this summer and this year I have been women's lacrosse club president for Newcastle.

I'm going to Australia to work and then travel New Zealand and South East Asia. Then the following year I have a place on a Masters at Reading University to do real estate.

Maddie Hudson I have had an amazing third year at university. Elected as welfare representative for Loughborough Students Dance Club, I managed to raise £4,000 for our chosen charity Young Minds, through the creation of my own mental health campaign called Love Your Mind. This campaign has encouraged AU sports teams and the Vice Chancellor of the University to open up about mental health within sport. With studies coming to an end, I have just set up my own drama school in Surrey, with classes starting in August this year. I have thoroughly enjoyed my time at Loughborough and am looking forward to the future.

Eleanor Murphy I will be graduating this summer from Loughborough University with a degree in Geography, and I am hoping to extend my studies further and will be doing a masters over the coming year.

Eleanor Parsonage I am now a second-year fashion student at Falmouth University taking this year much more seriously than the last and currently making a men's and women's collection based on nineties riot girl feminists combined with the Catholic Church.

Freja Petrie I have loved working at university, and I am hoping now to get a job in my year out before returning to my studies in London.

Charlotte Price I will be graduating this summer from Falmouth University with a First, and I have loved every moment I have been in Falmouth. I am currently hoping to be moving across the pond to New York City and to work in events and business. I will be going back to Cancer Research UK this summer to help train the new event assistants for the South Team.

Francesca Quince I have recently left my job in Oxford and will be moving to London this summer and I am excited to be working in the city.

Hannah Reichwald I'm in my second year studying Theatre and Performance at Falmouth. I still haven't learnt to surf but am really loving life down here. After university I intend to create a theatre company which focuses on theatre in education.

Trudi Seager I'm on my year abroad at the moment in Barcelona because I study Catalan and Spanish. Absolutely loving it and excited to go into my final year next year!

Jane Seymour Currently enjoying second year BA Hons Art History and Fine Art at Kingston School of Art. Hoping to embark on a summer internship in central London.

Hannah Southam I am currently working at London Scottish House and have been there for the last year and a half. I have been given a promotion (my boss still hasn't decided on a title yet as it's a new role). Recently had my ACL (ligament) reconstructed so I'm currently on the road to recovery and doing really well.

Section 84 (2015)
Section Representative:
Stephanie Thorndyke

Over the 2018 summer I worked with PGL in Brighton, it was beautiful, and I loved living in the South East. I then worked for a restaurant here in Bristol before heading back out to the Alps for the ski season, this time in Kuhtai, Austria. My season came to an early end due to personal reasons, but I am back home again (for now) before hopefully going back for the ski season at the start of April with **Ella** and then to Corsica or Mallorca for the summer season.

Best Asvasirayothin is currently in her third and final year at Central St Martins, graduating in July 2019. She will then be taking a masters degree at Sotheby's Institute of Art in New York to read Art, Law & Business.

Leila Dzhalilova says that life has changed dramatically since last year as she moved to Saint Petersburg last September to study Theory of Translation at Saint Petersburg State University. Studying at SPSU helped her to realise that what she is passionate about is learning languages. She is currently on her first year, having worked for two years before applying to university. The main languages on her course are English, Spanish and Chinese and she also keeps on improving her Turkish. The city has given her an opportunity to meet so many amazing people that it is hard to feel homesick!

Ella Frowen is currently finishing another ski season in the Alps as a private chef and has been offered a position in Mallorca for the summer as a private villa chef.

Yemi Greene is in her final year at the University of Durham and is hoping to take a gap year working and travelling. She sees **Katherine (Section 85)** a lot and they play lacrosse against each other.

Kelsey Heath will graduate from Ohio Wesleyan University with a Bachelor of Arts degree in Psychology, with a History minor. In September she is going to attend Quest Professional in London, after which she will look to join the workplace.

Phoebe Lowes has graduated from RAU and since then has been working in a wide range of jobs. She is now, and for the foreseeable future, working in estate management.

Lucy Marsh completed her three-year degree at Cardiff University graduating with a BMus. A week after completing her degree she went to Java, Indonesia, for three weeks with Cardiff University's Gamelan and did workshops with the University of Solo and surrounding Gamelan groups. She is still playing with a group in Gloucestershire and hopes to pursue her studies of Gamelan drumming in the future. At the moment she is having a year off working as an Assistant Housemistress and Music Graduate back at Westonbirt. Next year she plans to do her Teacher's Training in Music.

Elizabeth Motley graduated in Practical Film-making last year and is currently living in London. She has a job in artist development in the music industry; she is working on online content creation, social media management and music videos. She still sees **Tomi, Daisy** and **Lucy** often.

Becky Murphy has recently moved back to Wiltshire to be closer to her family. On 1st March she gave birth to a little girl called Alice who weighed 7.5lbs. She is absolutely beautiful, and both mother and baby are doing really well… Congratulations!

Rosie Nagle graduated last year from the RAU and got a first! She has had to do a bit of job-hopping but at the moment she is working for an online jeweller, and in a few months she will hopefully be buying her first house with her boyfriend.

Mollie Prince moved to London after graduating from the RAU and is now working for Caprice Holdings helping organise events in the private rooms at The Ivy, The Club at The Ivy and 34 Mayfair and is really enjoying it.

Tilly White is currently working as a chef at Chez Bruce in Wandsworth.

Section 83 (2014)
Section Representative:
Amelie Sievers

Ruby Chan I have been studying a Masters degree in Architecture at the University of Manchester. It is a three-year course but after twelve months in Manchester, I will probably return to Hong Kong to work while studying part-time to continue the course via distance learning.

Bryony Curry I graduated from Cardiff University last summer with a first in Biomedical Physiology and was awarded the best undergraduate research project by the Physiological Society. I went on to present a poster of my project at the Physiological Society conference in London and received the Rob Clarke Award which was great! I am now doing an MPhil at Cardiff Metropolitan University in Comparative Physiology. I am involved with the International Primate Heart Project which is interested in cardiovascular health in primates. As part of this, I've gone to some zoos in the UK and went to Chimfunshi Chimpanzee Sanctuary last December which was amazing! I also moved in with my boyfriend last summer and persuaded him to adopt a stray cat. She's lovely but slightly crazy at times!

Eloise Fitzmaurice I am still at Durham University studying a Masters in Risk (as in terrorism and security and not the board game!) after somehow graduating from my Geography degree in June with a first. I'm still down at the track four times a week doing 200/400m sprinting and also run a circuit class every week. I am also still running the not-for-profit organisation Cyber Champions as a Durham University Volunteering Project. My volunteers and I have now delivered Cyber Safety workshops to over a thousand school pupils in the Durham area and my deputy and I are hoping to deliver a parent workshop soon. Other than that, I was put in charge of organising Freshers' Week for all the new postgraduates at my Durham College, St Mary's, which was very tiring but great fun! I currently have no idea what I am doing next year, but hopefully I'll find something enjoyable.

Jessica Honer I am now in my final semester at university concentrating on Fine Art now, having done Photography as well previously. I am currently working hard towards the end-of-year degree show for which I am producing a short film as well as making 3D installations, a completely new area for me. Life after university is still uncertain but I am hoping to enter the property world.

Emily McGuire I am currently at Bristol University studying Forensic Computing and Security. During my spare time I have created my own freelance writing business, as well as being published, blogging and hosting my own podcast. The majority of my work is in favour of equal rights for women and the LGBTQIA+ community.

Louise Nicholls The last twelve months have been quite busy for me. After being a part of the launch of shopDisney, I was promoted to Disney Destinations International as an operations coordinator. However, after a few months there I was approached by the civil service and I am now a policy advisor in the Department for Business, Energy and Industrial Strategy on everyone's favourite topic... EU Exit (sorry in advance!). Nothing however can prepare you from seeing an old Westonbirt teacher in a government canteen (hi, Mr Burkinshaw!)

Khadijah Ismail I am currently doing a Masters in Energy Management at ESCP Europe Business School in London. I will be moving to the Paris Campus in April to finish off the last three months. After that I intend to do an internship in management consulting at McKinsey & Company while writing my thesis for my course.

Amelia Schiller I work for Trafalgar Entertainment, a theatre production company based in London, as an office coordinator which enables me to tackle both administrative responsibilities but also largely production-based tasks. I am incredibly proud to say that the company has just been nominated for twelve Olivier nominations for shows that I have worked closely on and I can't wait to see what else we are able to accomplish.

Amelie Sievers I am in the final year of my Psychology degree and this year has by far been my favourite! I got to be the student representative at Exeter for all things Wellbeing and have been really happy with all the changes I have been able to make this year, which are really influencing university strategy. I have also been a Trustee of the Students' Guild here and have absolutely loved making strategic decisions and representing students at the highest level; I am currently involved in recruiting for a new

CEO which has been really fascinating. I am still leading an Eating Disorders support group which has been so interesting and I am really thankful for all the opportunities I've had here at Exeter.

Kristina Smith I have just finished my final university thesis (like a dissertation) a couple of months ago and I am currently doing an international environmental law internship in Budapest for six months - loving every second of it!

Alice Wordsworth: I have been having a brilliant time living and studying in London. I'm living in Vauxhall with Exeter mates and the wonderful **Georgie Fenn**, which makes it a very happy house! I got offered a place on Birkbeck's MFA in Theatre Directing, a course I had held in high esteem, with only ten of us in the class. It has proved to be the most brilliant platform and I feel so honoured to be studying there. Each week we have visiting directors and playwrights in to talk to us about their work. I feel in awe every day of the people I am meeting and have forged amazing new friendships. Last term I was on placement at the Drama Centre, which was an intense but fascinating experience. We are now applying for our placements next year, which will be a year long and in theatres across the country. I am loving studying again and feel very lucky to be learning about the thing I love every day.

Sophie Wu I finished my masters degree at LSE last year and I am now working at China Life Insurance (Overseas) in Hong Kong as an Assistant Actuarial Analyst. I am hoping that I will learn a lot on my first job.

Sally Yau I am currently doing my pre-registration pharmacist training year at Boots and will be attending my pre-registration exam at the end of June. Hopefully I will pass the exam and get a job in London as a pharmacist!

Section 82 (2013)
Section Representative:
Abi Lowes

Saskia Burden I'm still at Liverpool University and six years down in my life as an eternal student! I'm now in my third year of Veterinary and in my last year of lectures as I will be starting my two years of clinical rotations this time next year over at our Leahurst campus on the Wirral. I'm in full swing of clinical placements outside term time and absolutely loving the farm and equine practice that I see. Also, I will be spending part of September in an absolutely enormous three-year, million-pound research study into dairy cow lameness; the results could have a massive impact on the industry which to me is pretty exciting stuff!

Lucy Fenn I am still with the Crown Prosecution Service, managing the North London Crown Courts, but after a month in Australia I'll be starting as the Area's Communication Manager for the CPS. I am now a yoga teacher as well. I qualified last year in Greece and now teach at One LDN each Friday, have private clients and host yoga brunches and charity events at the weekend and just love it! Still living in Fulham and soaking up every second.

Alice Fyfe I have done some travelling in South America over the last year and now I'm training to be a nurse at King's College London. At present I'm on placement at St Mary's Paddington on a vascular surgery ward. It's intense and long hours but I really do love it.

Emma Gardner I started my PhD in English Literature in October last year, three days after the final deadline of my masters. I graduated from the Masters in Crime and Gothic Fictions in early February this year, where I was valedictorian, which was an immense honour. Alongside postgraduate studies I've helped organise and run international conferences and will be presenting a paper at a conference in Italy this summer.

Cassie Greenhill I'm still working in offshore wind. In July I moved off the graduate scheme into a role as a Consent Manager (onshore/offshore planning and environmental management), which can be very challenging at times but I'm enjoying it! I've been keeping up with lacrosse playing for Cheltenham and we have tournaments at Westonbirt.

Gemma Harborne I finished my PR degree and got a 2:1, and then went off to travel Central America which was incredible. I'm now doing a Masters in Vocal Performance, Music Composition and Production at Leeds College of Music and loving it. Hoping to become a professional singer-songwriter, and after this year I would like to do some travelling whilst performing and song-writing abroad.

Hester Ingram I have moved away from the marketing world and am now working at Arriva Rail London assisting on a major project to modernise the London Overground with TfL I've learned more about trains than I thought I would ever need to but so far, I am really enjoying it.

Annabel Jardine-Blake This last year I have finished my masters at Kings College London and got my first full time job in the NHS. I work in an adolescent psychiatric inpatient ward and am loving it. It's really hard work and incredibly stressful at times but it's so rewarding and it's great to have a job I enjoy.

Abigail Lowes In September last year I started a Garden Design course which I have almost finished and am looking to go on to the diploma level this coming September. I am really enjoying the course and all the horticulture I am learning.

Izzy Lysaght I've been busy in a new job forging a career in niche IT recruitment. My boss is showing me the ropes and I'm really enjoying it so far.

Lydia Marshall I am working in finance still, having spent the last few months specialising in investment consulting. Other than that, I am living in a flat in Bristol and enjoying life to the full!

Georgie Mobbs I'm still working at Wirth Research but now as a Project Manager, responsible for our refrigeration projects in the US. Getting to travel out there a fair bit, which is fun! Work keeps me busy at the moment, and when I'm not working, I'm continuing with my HNC in General Engineering.

Lexi Noon I am now working as an enterprise sales representative for a tech company called BlueJeans. Its HQ is in San Francisco which is great as I get to travel to the US.

Laura Snape I am enjoying my time at the University of Westminster, doing my Masters in Architecture and working alongside a practice in Surrey.

Fiona Vincent I graduated with a Bachelor of Medicine, Bachelor of Surgery from the University of Southampton in July 2018. I started working as a Foundation Doctor in Poole Hospital in August. I am really enjoying living and working in Poole. Life as a junior doctor is busy, but I love what I do. I am also the Foundation Trainee Representative for all hospitals in the Wessex region. In my spare time I enjoy running, water sports and travelling as well as catching up with friends.

Section 81 (2012)
Section Representative:
Olivia Birkin-Hewitt

No news returned this year

Section 80 (2011)
Section Representative:
Emily Clare

No news returned this year

Section 79 (2010)
Section Representative:
Sophie Martin

No news returned this year

Section 78 (2009)
Section Representative:
Amy Falkenburg

No news returned this year

Section 77 (2008)
Section Representative:
Portia Ingram

Sophia Barker moved to Hong Kong in August 2018 to be a founding staff member at Malvern College, Hong Kong. She is now teaching Prep 2 as well as being housemistress for Elgar House. If any Westonbirt girls find themselves in Hong Kong and would like to meet up with a friendly face, please feel free to contact her. She still speaks regularly with all her

Westonbirt friends and is very excited about celebrating the forthcoming weddings of **Tessa Moreland** and **Lottie Sharland**.

Mary-Jane Collinson Mudge has secured a post in further speciality training in geriatrics which will begin in August 2019 and she has been nominated colleague of the year at her current hospital. She still lives in the Yorkshire Dales with her boyfriend Justin, dog Billy and many lovely pets.

Emma Glynn is still working for Gloucestershire Fire and Rescue Service as a PA. She is awaiting her results of her Chartered Management Institute Level 5 course in Leadership and Management. She is currently in the process of planning a travelling trip next year across parts of Europe. Emma still lives with her boyfriend, Ed, in Gloucester.

Portia Ingram is currently living in Putney with her two sisters (**Rosie** and **Hester**) and undertook a career change last year, moving away from marketing; she now works as an Executive Assistant in the City of London, within the finance sector, which she is really enjoying. She still sees lots of Westonbirt friends and is looking forward to being a bridesmaid for **Lottie Sharland** in October and attending **Tessa Moreland's** wedding in September. Portia organised a ten-year reunion for her section last April which was well attended and enjoyed by all!

Tessa Moreland is currently looking to move back to London having been away travelling with her fiancé, Rich Oliver, and spending the last few months skiing in the mountains. She still sees lots of her Westonbirt friends and looks forward to being a bridesmaid for **Lottie Sharland** and getting married herself in September. The wedding will take place in Gloucestershire.

Rosie Margesson is currently living in Tooting and works in publishing in London. She regularly sees the Westonbirt girls from her year and is looking forward to the upcoming weddings for **Lottie Sharland** and **Tessa Moreland** and being a bridesmaid to them both.

Louisa North Louisa is currently working for a small start-up called the British Game Alliance, which has been set up to promote British feathered game and to self-regulate the shooting industry. She is working as the Executive Assistant to the Managing Director and Office Manager.

Charlotte Sharland Lottie is currently living in central London with her sister **Clemmie** and still works in marketing. She is engaged to Dan

Mayland and they are getting married in Dorset this October. Lottie has chosen a few Westonbirt girls she is close to as her bridesmaids and can't wait for the wedding!

Section 76 (2007)

Section Representative:
New Representative needed
(Report from Jane Reid – Section 30)

Only those with email addresses were contacted.

Section 75 (2006)

Section Representative:
Charlotte Boyes

Emma Barlow (Febry) Living near Horton with my husband and two-year-old son Solomon. Working in social care.

Charlotte Boyes I am living between London and the Cotswolds working as a veterinary surgeon, and have a miniature French bulldog called Dot. Awarded the certificate for advanced veterinary practice in 2018, I am about to undertake an MBA. My small online equestrian business is attending Badminton Horse Trials and Blenheim Horse Trials this year, so it would be lovely to say hello.

Elle Brindley (Ewan) I am living near Winchester with my husband and three-year-old daughter Annabelle and our fluffy cat Otis. Teaching ALevel Psychology at Winchester College.

Millie Gallagher (Jenkin) I've been living in Morzine in the French Alps for two years, doing as much skiing, hiking and indulging in cheese as possible! I married Doug in October last year with a small ceremony in Suffolk, and we are looking forward to moving back to the UK (Cirencester area) this summer.

Wendy Hagues (Browne) After finishing a PhD at the University of Cambridge, I started a lecturing-based role at the university. I am teaching masters and undergraduate students in the field of Psychology and

Education. I am married to Edward Hagues and we have a one-year-old daughter called Audrey.

Emma Logan After seven years in London I have now relocated to Bath with my fiancé, Tom. I am making a move from sales to consultancy, helping companies recruit the right people. We are also busy planning our 2019 winter wedding!

Emily Sayer I am living near Taunton with my three-year-old daughter Aubrey and managing my own accounting firm.

Susanna Steele (Mayo) I am working as a civil servant and got married in June 2016 at Westonbirt House! We have a little girl, Annabella, who will be two in April.

Pamela Turner (Moth) My fiancée returned from Afghanistan whereupon we got married in Somerset. We took a six-week honeymoon travelling around New Zealand and Samoa during which time my now husband was offered a job in Sierra Leone. Before the close of 2018, we relocated to Freetown.

Hannah Wheeler (Cunild) I am living in Bristol with my husband and my chocolate cocker spaniel. I have recently started my own CGI Design company (computer generated imagery) and I also work creating adverts, brochures and print.

Section 74 (2005)
Section Representative:
New Representative needed
(Report from Jane Reid – Section 30)

Only those with email addresses were contacted

There were no replies from any of the 10 email addresses to which messages were sent.

Section 73 (2004)
Section Representative:
Emily Paul (Stephenson)

No news returned this year

Section 72 (2003)
Section Representative:
Fiona Tubbs

Catherine Booth (Pritchard) lives in Perthshire with her husband and seven-month-old son and is currently on maternity leave from Savills where she works as a land agent.

Olivia Cameron Livvy is completing her diploma in zoo-keeping (and avoiding meerkat bites) and is also due to marry later this year.

Anna Yau Chan (Chan) is back in Hong Kong and currently a full-time mum of two. She recently did a European trip.

Lillian Drury noted that ten years ago she was just returning from Helmand in Afghanistan but now works in the luxury travel industry, visiting some slightly different locations, mainly focused on skiing.

Genevieve Foote Genny lives back in the USA running an associate degree programme at a local community college. She also plays ultimate frisbee, including volunteering at the World Flying Disc Federation World Ultimate Club Championships last year.

Svenja Fromman is head of therapy at a hospital and currently on lives in Hamburg with her boyfriend and eleven-month-old son.

Chloe Hennessey Kitt is a very busy bee living in Brighton and working as an actor, artist, performer and entertainer.

Octavia Higginson (Perry-Adlam) Ocky is currently lives in Bristol with her two nippers who keep her busy.

Lotta Kockum has a long-term boyfriend and is living back in Stockholm working as a doctor, specialising in work with children and young people, which includes a project promoting physical activity to prevent depression and anxiety.

Caroline Lambert (McMeekin) Kitsy is currently on maternity leave with sprog number two and head of Creative Arts at a London School.

Zoe Lester (Hatherell) is living in Washington DC with her husband and eleven-month-old daughter, working as an actuary; she is managing a team in auto insurance, via a PhD which involved a stint in Geneva at the particle collider.

Anastasia Lisyutina Nastia lives near Maidenhead with her husband, four-year-old daughter and her cat. She works for an in-house recruitment company.

Carey Milsom (Logan) lives near Malmesbury with her husband and eighteen-month-old daughter and is working at Bath Hospital as part of the oncology clinical trials team.

Florence Richardson (Warrington) lives in rural Ireland with her husband, two daughters, a dog and too many sheep.

Amina Tofa is back in Nigeria and worked as a pharmacist, then lectured, and is currently being kept busy looking after her three boys.

Fiona Tubbs is a litigation lawyer working in Birmingham, whilst honing her circus skills in the evening.

Corinna Turner is writing and publishing books with a following both in the UK and America and travels from place to place in her campervan.

Eleonore Vandoorne Ellie is an artist and was nominated for the Royal Arts Prize earlier this year. She got married last year and is also currently engaged on a huge property restoration project, with her husband, in France.

Prunella Walker Prue is currently embarking on training to become a mental health nurse and lives in Scotland with her boyfriend and cat, who is not quite a dog...

Lucilla Welchman (Hickie) Lucy lives in the lovely West Sussex countryside with her husband and two children and is currently on a break from teaching.

Section 71 (2002)
Section Representative:
Joanna Colson

Caroline Chan Still in same job and living in HK! I have a one-and-a-half-year-old boy.

Viola Chan I'm still in HK and my daughter just turned two.

Narisa Cherdjareewatananun I'm currently working as a freelance consultant for interiors styling and retails visual branding. Left my full-time job a month ago. Also working on my dinnerware collection launching end of this year.

Jo Colson Still working for the same family as a nanny/PA. Have set up my own babysitting agency for childcare for events in the Cotswolds.

Hattie Coverdale (Fisher) Still in same job. I have a six-month-old and still live in London.

Lucinda Dalton Still living in London and started a new job in a Mayfair gallery as head of sales in September. Hope everyone is well.

Julia Grant All much the same with me - still living in London and working as a label manager at a record label.

Alice Lycett Green Much the same for me, still working in marketing for a children's charity and we have our eighteen-month-old daughter keeping us busy too.

Olivia Mulholland I'm still working for a renewable energy supplier and now studying for an accreditation in process improvement. Living in Badminton.

Amy Oswin (Pounder) I'm the compliance manager for Innovate UK, UKRI - also running around after Samuel, who's now almost eighteen months old.

Lovisa Pahlson-Moller Still living in London with Freddie (10), Ollie (4) and a new dog. Studying for a diploma in ADHD and starting my first big interior design project.

Clem Paine (Boulton) We're still living in Hampshire. We welcomed Ralph, a little brother for Tabitha, at the end of November.

Lucie Wright (Collinson) I'm still living in London, got married to husband Charlie in 2016. I have recently completed my medical specialty training in public health.

Section 70 (2001)
Section Representative:
Catharine Loveridge (Hallpike)

Amelia Annfield It's been a busy and wonderful year. It's my fifth year as a freelancer and still going strong! I remain based at my studio in Hackney Downs and continue to work as art director for film, tv and events.

I've been involved in many projects including London Design Week and Paris Deco Week, and I was commissioned by The Rug Company to create and build fabric installations at their showrooms. I also worked on The Greatest Dancer on the BBC earlier this year and helped create the sets for the ITV show Small Fortune.

I made an exciting trip to Kenya and South Africa last year and I am heading to Marrakesh and Istanbul for inspiration this year - to source and buy and hopefully do some photography. Please see some of my most recent projects on www.ameliaannfield.co.uk.

Hermione Harbutt (Berry) I am living in Bristol with my husband and two-year-old daughter. Continuing to run my Couture Accessory business (Hermione Harbutt) from two locations, Clifton in Bristol and Kensington in London. It has been lovely to continue my role as Westonbirt Champion again this year, speaking to the students about life as a female entrepreneur and designer.

Fiona MacFarlane (Cameron) I am living in Aberdour, Scotland with my husband Jamie and little girl Amalie, expecting another new arrival at the end of May.

I have set up a business selling illustrations and art commissions and had my first illustrated children's book published just before Christmas, currently working on the next two instalments!

Maija Calvert is writing this from Delhi, India...

I moved to Paris from London in 2015 to work in the Children's House (three-to-six years) at the Beautiful Minds École Montessori Internationale. I then realised my passion is working with toddlers and am working in a Bilingual Infant Community at the school, speaking English to the children (and trying not to speak French!) and following and guiding the natural rhythms of the two-to-three-year olds. I am going to do another exciting AMI Montessori Diploma over two summer holidays (in London at the Maria Montessori Institute).

*AMI: Dr Maria Montessori founded the Association Montessori Internationale to protect her research and work. An AMI Diploma is valuable across the world.

Rose Farquhar I've been Head of Partnerships for Nyetimber, England's finest sparkling wine producers, for two and a half years now, travelling all over the globe marketing the brand, whilst also very much enjoying my hobby of singing at lots of events.

Pippa Bremner (Goodwin Self) I am teaching and living in Buckinghamshire. Our little boy is growing fast, and we are loving every second.

Catherine Loveridge (Hallpike) I am still living in Suffolk teaching English at Orwell Park School and looking after the girls the rest of the time! My elder daughter, Rose, started Reception in September - I don't feel nearly grown up enough to have a child at school!

Tor Jones-Davies(Inskip) Well, my news is baby based! I had a baby girl, Eliza, in December, our first child. We are living near Malmesbury and I am enjoying maternity leave. That's about the size of it!

Ellie Harrington (Street) Ellie is still living in Tunbridge Wells, with both boys now at school, and an energetic puppy. She runs a digital marketing company specialising in social media campaigns.

Abby Moule (Warn) This year we moved to the Cotswolds north of Cirencester. Scarlett has started school and Seraphina starts this September. Everyone is well and there is little drama, life is good!

Phillippa Dalby-Welsh (Warrington) Nick and I were thrilled to welcome Henrietta Dalby-Welsh into the world in Nov 2017. I took 9 months maternity leave and in March 2018 we went on a family road trip around Europe, visiting Belgium, Germany, Austria and France for a month. Hettie is now fifteen months old and very busy!

I went back to work full-time in September last year, and Nick has taken on more of the domestic responsibilities. He now spends two days a week looking after Hettie and does the nursery pick-ups/drop-offs on the three mid-week days. The balance seems to be working well. I am still at Savills and took over a regional role in January this year, as co-head of Prime Central London. If Westonbirt ever wants a spokesperson for a careers day to talk about what it's like in the world of property, I'd be delighted to come along for a chat.

Section 69 (2000)
Section Representative:
Lucy Croysdill (Fletcher)

Laura Arnott (Griffiths) I am married to Stephen and I'm a stay-at-home mum to Henry and Elizabeth. We are currently living in Biloxi, Mississippi, but about to move to Alexandria, Virginia. I try to get back to the UK every year and stay in touch with a few girls from my year, mainly Lucy and Michelle.

Lucy Croysdill (Fletcher) I am enjoying life in Tunbridge Wells and working from home. Nina is now in Year 1 and enjoying all that school offers. We recently visited Westonbirt with **Michelle Lawson** and she couldn't believe the size of 'Mummy's school'.

Lucinda Dungarvan (Davy) Rory and I welcomed Tatiana in August, she is wonderful and very happy, a big but exciting change to start our family. We remain living in London and, whilst I am on maternity leave, I am still working for the same family office.

Clemmie Jacques I have obtained my doctorate in Counselling Psychology and am now working in several roles. I work for the NHS in an early intervention for psychosis unit in Hackney, I also work as a private therapist for The Priory in the City. In addition to this, I have published my research and presented it at nationwide conferences in Psychology. I am also a regular guest lecturer, on a range of topics, at City University and St. Mary's University and am considered to be a specialist in gender identity, psychosis, online therapeutic interventions, addictions, multiculturalism and service user empowerment. I have also started consulting for media projects such as plays, films and television shows. Finally, I run several wellbeing retreats in Turkey each year for women in recovery.

Section 68 (1999)
Section Representative:
New Representative needed
(Report compiled by Jane Reid – Section 30)

Only those with email addresses were contacted

Isla Richardson acknowledged the AGM 2019 notice.

Section 67 (1998)
Section Representative:
Julia Collis (Bleasdale)

Julia Collis (Bleasdale) Since last year we have continued to settle into our new village and the children enjoyed returning to school in September as more established Kingswood pupils. It has been wonderful to make new friends and watch as the new relationships grow for the children. Our life revolves around school activities, matches and kids' parties but that is hugely enjoyable, and I love being able to be around for this. I have got a part time job at Monkton Prep School, which is keeping me out of trouble. It is super to have another focus and I feel very lucky that they have allowed me to keep a good balance between work and home. I continue to work for a very inspiring family whose son, Jonathan Bryan, has written a book with his eyes called, *Eye Can Write*; if you get a chance I would definitely recommend reading his book

Section 66 (1997)
Section Representative:
Katie Mason (Eves)

Hannah Armstrong (Busby) This last year, I have had my second baby. Ziggy Roy Armstrong. He is now ten months old and I have recently gone back to work. Still in the same job, working as a homeware buyer and product developer. Can't wait to see you all for the reunion on the farm!

Nellie Burroughes A busy couple of years has seen three house moves, and an eight-month-old Sam, and shows no signs of abating with lots of fun stunt work coming in along with planning our wedding in June. It's all go go go and fun fun fun!

Zarina Chatwin (Marsh) Back in London with all three children in school and a new puppy. Getting used to London living again.

Sally Cullum (Hopwell) Still managing the accounts for Boughton Estate in Northamptonshire and completed an eighth financial year end just before Christmas. Work progressing on our pretty Victorian house, but with all the wooden windows needing restoration this spring, it looks to be another busy year ahead of packing up rooms and decorating.

Siobhan Dunn (Suffield-Jones) I am still a lady of leisure being kept in the manner to which I have become accustomed by my husband and two children (Lydia now 8 and Jeremy 5), i.e. stressed up to my eyeballs and running around after them all!

Jess Green (White) We're ticking along. Life is pretty hectic with three small people and work but all good. Can't wait for a catch-up soon. If anyone is passing Swindon, pop in for a visit (and **Marina** only a few minutes away which is awesome).

Katie Mason (Eves) A rather grown-up year in the Mason household, now firmly on the upward trajectory. Cecily is now at school and loving it, Rosa is as hilarious as always and Will has just turned one and is a blissfully content little man. I was diagnosed with breast cancer last July, we moved back into our revamped house on the day of my first surgery. I had another surgery, recently finished chemo, so just radio and endocrine therapy to go; then I can pack it all in a box and forget about it. Ad and the children and **Hets** and **Marina** among many others have been amazing and a brilliant distraction but I'm looking forward to normality, growing some hair, and getting back to work in July.

Jo Ogilvy (Llewelyn) continues to live in Somerset, travel the country recruiting leaders for schools, and racing home to see husband, son and dog as quickly as possible! The new dog is the great excitement of the year, a border terrier from Swansea (obviously a pre-requisite that she was Welsh), and she's brought lots of happiness to the fold. Antony is at a primary school that is just about bigger than the one I went to, albeit only five other children in his year, and seems to be enjoying himself. It would be so lovely to see any of you if ever you are passing through Somerset on the way to Devon/Cornwall; we make a very convenient pit stop, living on the cut through from the A303 to the M5. I really do mean it.

Sam Vermaak (Russell) is still at the University of Oxford managing VALIDATE, an international network of scientists aiming to accelerate vaccine development for four diseases linked to poverty, which is an interesting and varied challenge. This year I also trained as a Business and Personal Coach so am setting up my own blog and business and really enjoying helping others be happier and more fulfilled in their lives. After twelve years of living in Oxfordshire I also finally learned to row this year! Still very happily married to Corné (unbelievably we celebrated our fifteenth year!) and we're packing as much adventure and travel into our lives as we can.

Claire Warman (Cathery) I have three boys aged 11, 9 and 6. They are all good. I live in Hampshire and have my own online clothing business www.bigcatclothing.com. Take a look!

Kate Young (Mahoney) I am still producing commercials for various advertising agencies in London, which keeps me happily globe-trotting. Always best when it's a winter sun location. We're doing the final phase of build work to our house in Catford. It's only taken ten years! Poppy is nearly eight and is enjoying Year 3 and is on the school council.

Section 65 (1996)
Section Representative:
Catherine Hirons (Charlton)

Sophie Bampton (Meredith) We have had a slightly uneventful year as well, till now. Just been working lots, and business is going well although I'm starting to feel my age now with the long days and late nights at the big jobs! Beau is three next month, which seems crazy. Time goes so fast these days. She is in nursery three days a week and then we just hang out the rest of the time. We are in Australia this whole month visiting her grandma, and she is in heaven here. It is insanely hot and we don't have any air-conditioning! This year we plan do to more travel before she starts school. I hope everyone else is well. I haven't seen much of anyone this year, but I have seen **Charlie** a couple of times. I try and stay in touch with **Susie** and **Frances** a little bit. Just a quiet year all round.

Alexandra Butler (Earley) Still living in Sherston and working for myself. Enjoying lots more time with my two girls (now 8 and 6) and time to pursue some other interests. Just completed some renovation work and glad to no longer be living in a building site. Looking forward to some warmer weather.

Louisa Gallimore Nothing much to report this year - I suppose no news is good news! Audrey is nearly three and starts her first year at our local French Maternelle this year and Sam is six and will start primary school; I can't believe how fast time is going! We're making the most of being near the snow and have been up skiing a few times already this year, had a wonderful Christmas in Australia, and other than that just work, work, work! As always would be lovely to see anyone who finds themselves in the south of France. I hope everyone is well and happy.

Emily Haslam (Marshall) This year has been a crazy one - full of love and happiness. Not only did we adopt two hairy scruffy terriers but literally a month later our baby girl came along! We have adopted the most beautiful baby girl, Gracie, who together with our doggies has changed our lives immeasurably for the better. Such a wonderful and amazing surprise having been on the waiting list for years - she really is the happiest and sweetest little lady full of smiles and giggles. Luckily the office gave me a few months maternity leave and so I spent a very happy few months playing - mostly trying to stop Gracie chewing the dog toys and the puppy from chewing Gracie's toys. It has been hilarious and our home is happily destroyed! My poor husband, his quiet peaceful life totally in tatters, which he is loving too. Now back at work and for the first time in my life planning my daily escape by noon or activating my work-from-home strategy to ensure I don't miss a second of first steps, first word or first anything! Although it is sometimes a relief to sit behind my desk with a large cappuccino.

Caroline Kearsley (White) We are all still in Cornwall, dealing with a toddler and a teenager and one in between. Honey choose her GCSEs and is fighting me as to which parties she can go to, while I sniff her clothes for the smell of alcohol or cigarettes. This does remind me a lot of us as thirteen-year olds. I am also a bit of a dance mum too, travelling to competitions with **Amelie**, that I secretly really enjoy. Lara has just turned two and is a curly-haired ball of energy. Hopefully doing a bit of camping in France this summer and hanging out here. Lots of love to you all x

Isabel Langly-Smith (Lowndes) As my youngest started school in September, it suddenly dawned on me that I really did want to work again. So, I am now back at my prep school running their marketing and communications; I am loving it and my kids are all at the school too which is great. Working full-time is a bit of a shock, but so far so good - and half-term is round the corner!

Harriet Mackinlay (Bradley) Louis Nicholas John Mackinlay was born on 22/4/18 and he's just gorgeous! I've just gone back to work two days a week for March and Bert has taken shared parental leave for the month so it's a nice gentle start and I am beginning to feel a bit more on top of things again. Can't believe the year has gone by so fast, it's been unbelievably tough but so incredibly rewarding (mums out there - I feel so bad I never realised what it was like before!). We loved seeing **Fliss** and meeting Louis's newest little friend Margot.

Alys Mathew Not too many changes over the last year; like everyone else celebrated four decades on this planet but did it in my own way. Took on one challenge to mark each decade split into mental, physical, overcoming a fear (heights) and creative. Absolutely loved it and can now say I have cycled across the width of Italy in a day (sunrise to sunset, 274km, 4.5k meters climbing), raced at Ironman 70.3 World Championships in South Africa (eight fastest in the world in our age group), climbed Mont Blanc (4,808m and highest mountain in Western Europe) and did a day's cookery course at Le Manoir Aux Quat'Saisons. All of them were epic in their own way - not sure how 2019 is going to top that!

Hannah Pope (West) Still in Somerset and loving it. The kids are both in school now and I've started a little body/face and hair oil business - trading at the fantastic local markets and festivals around us. There are lots of small hand-made businesses around here and it's really fun to be involved.

Una Strauss (Laffan) Living in Bayswater, London. Still teaching yoga one-to-ones and women's group classes. I also facilitate other spaces for women pre- and post-natal and a technique called Non-Linear Movement. Two gorgeous girls called Grace and Tara, 4 and nearly 3, are the best thing ever in my life, along with husband Jamie! Love to all.

Frances Von Bonde (Glyn-Owen) 2018 was a very busy year for us. We moved house in January and immediately renovated, which took ten weeks of dust, sweat and tears and then in July lovely Skyla was born. She's an awesome little soul and absolutely adored by Ella, which makes life somewhat easier as I've heard some horror stories. If another baby wasn't enough, we got a German Shepherd puppy, Echo, to add into the mix. He's one month younger than Skyla so two babies to attend to = never a dull moment. I spent the rest of the year juggling baby, puppy, three-year-old, sorting house, managing our rental properties and generally being run off my feet! Justin is away quite a bit at the moment, he's up near the Namibian border but loving his job so we can't complain. I started working for a small travel company at the beginning of this year and my hope is when things settle a bit more here (wishful thinking) it will take me into Africa on some adventures. Otherwise life is really good!

Jo Wilkie I've had a frustrating year sport wise as a hip injury has put me out of action from any major running and I've not competed in a year. Thankfully it doesn't affect my cycling so I've been doing a lot of bike miles and can compete at that. I'm currently training for a long-distance mountain event in the Dolomites, called Maratona, as well as short distance time trialling competitions. Probably double Dutch to most people, who I'm sure think I am insane, but actually, in my opinion, it is sport and competing that keeps me sane! I also use it as an excuse to travel and so am regularly off abroad, competing or on training trips and taking the opportunity of visiting other places.

Other travels have been snowboarding and a long weekend in Amsterdam at the end of last year, where we went to a Prodigy gig, which was totally mental, but one of their last after the sad news of Keith taking his life so feel lucky we got to see them. Things like that make you realise that life is precious and to make the most of it. I think I'm feeling old; what with most of us turning forty last year, or even the year before, it seems so odd, and genuinely the days of Sedgwick seem like just the other day.

I was back at Westonbirt last year for a 10k race, which I couldn't do due to injury, but I still went along to support some friends, but more so that I could have a good snoop about! Ate fish and chips in the main dining room, snuck up to Holford and Badminton and also down to the Lower Dining Room and Hades! Hades is still the same, even the smell... no joke!

Last year I was writing my resignation from my job and I am pleased to say that it all went to plan and so I've been in my current role nearly a year. I'm still in financial services, now working for a new insurance company in the market called Guardian. It's been exciting being part of a start-up, although a roller coaster of emotions at times and not without pressures. Fingers crossed that the business establishes itself and grows to be successful. I don't want to be writing about another change in a year's time.

Still enjoying village life with Dave and Hobbes, although Hobbes is probably as frustrated at the lack of running as I am. Although Dave and I met through our athletic club, he has also suffered with injury and had to switch to cycling which doesn't quite work the same for the dog!

Section 64 (1995)
Section Representative:
Emma Lloyd-Williams (Leek)

No news returned this year

Section 63 (1994)
Section Representative:
Belle Morton

Bryonie Clarendon (Leask) Living in Hampshire with George and the three boys, Edward, Freddie and Cosmo, running my own business.

Jess Ingham (Hipwood) Still living in Bristol, working for Orange as a Global Brand manager. Lots of travel, so far this year Egypt and Jordan, and Paris every other week. Started running last year and ran a half marathon which reminded me of those awful cross-country runs we used to do. Have now given up running, and acquired a dog, so dogwalking instead!

Emily Johnson I am still alive, kicking, well and happy with the same rebellious streak and very grey hair.

Nancy Lawson (White) I am still running the B&B and meeting venue at home; it is slightly chaotic with children and animals! But guests seem to enjoy staying and two businesses in Swindon have meetings here most weeks with a home cooked lunch served in the kitchen and my naughty Jack Russell trying to join team building events. Never a dull moment but, luckily, I work with a great team. I have just come back from Colombia which was incredible and I hope to travel lots more! Please come and stay or call in if you are passing. We are just off the M4.

Mary McCarthy (Oakes) Living in Cheltenham with three boys, Ollie, Monty and Zac, oh, and one husband! Whilst juggling my time as wife and mum I am still running my business off my laptop with weekly visits to London and getting involved in various other art dealing adventures both nationally and internationally. I am currently organising a massive Street Art exhibition with Bristol Council at the MShed in Bristol for 2020 called Vanguard Bristol Street Art Past & Present which will open in June 2020 until October 2020. On the personal side of things, I have just learnt how to surf and spent the last six months being totally obsessed by my new sport, much to my husband's despair, he feels like a surf widow apparently!

Jemima Mann Based in the UK running my own business but continue to work overseas in New Zealand and Europe.

Belle Morton Left Hong Kong after five years, put all my belongings in storage and taken the last year off which has been absolute bliss. Currently working out where my next location will be but, in the meantime, been enjoying catching up with quite a few of you and seeing some more of Europe.

Sharifa Parker (Taylor) Working full time for an IT company based in the UK and US. My eldest daughter starts secondary school in September and her sister is only a year behind her. I keep in touch and still see several Westonbirt girls based in the UK and overseas.

Section 62 (1993)

Section Representative:
Caroline Copland

Caroline Copland: I have taken on the role of Section Rep, quite a tricky position while all in Section 62 seem to be scattered around the world without the luxury of time to share news.

I am a marketing consultant Monday to Wednesday working on a number of projects but primarily, at the time of writing, on a large regeneration scheme in Manchester. On Thursdays and Fridays, I am a psychotherapist in Clapham and spend most of my weekends as far from the metropolis as possible, normally climbing hills with Kiwi boyfriend.

Section 61 (1992)

Section Representative:
Coquita Mills

A few girls from Section 61 enjoyed the ninetieth birthday celebrations at Westonbirt in May 2018, namely **Cordelia Gover (Harries), Charlotte Haynes (Hunt), Virginia Kelly, Claire Galer (Dorman), Coquita Mills (Marsh)**. It was a super day and it was nice to meet up with girls remembered (and teachers) as well as those not! The day had a lovely atmosphere and many amusing memories were recalled.

In January, we received the very sad news that **Marissa Pilkington (Learmond)** lost her husband, Simon, after a battle with cancer. Old friends are keeping her and her family in their thoughts.

Angela Clark I am still working as a paediatric staff nurse at Addenbrooke's hospital but left the busy ward I was on after seventeen years and now work in paediatric recovery looking after the children following surgery. I am kept busy with my children's activities, and mentally preparing for my eldest going off to university in September. I wish everyone well.

Cordelia Gover (Harries) Not much news from me... just keeping busy with my girls Jazzy (10) & Ellie (8) and my many pets, alongside my property work and parish council duties. It's always lovely to keep up with Westonbirt and I enjoyed the ninetieth birthday party last summer with **Coquita, Virginia, Charlie,** and **Claire**. I've seen **Lina, Raqs** and **Marissa** over the year too.

Virginia Kelly I'm still living in Malvern with my other half and two children, Rufus who is just about to turn eight and Eleanor who is five. Time is flying! I'm working from home doing business affairs consultancy for television drama productions and doing a yoga teacher training course. Also renovating an old barn. So, life is pretty hectic this year. Have seen, or been in contact with, a few old Westonbirt girls which is always lovely!

Coquita Mills (Marsh) We finally finished some building work which was beyond tedious so am now looking for something to do when the children are at school. They are nine and five and require a lot of maintenance! All good fun. We are really settled into life in UK now though Simon jets about quite a bit which at least keeps me in gin. The garden party in June last year was a real treat.

Caroline Wilson (Pullin) All fine with me. Our two boys are growing up, now eleven and eight. They bring us a lot of fun. The farm still keeps us busy and we are about to start lambing again (probably said the same last year!) Mum is still with us, now 82, and still my rock for all advice, so wise and kind to us all. Sadly, we lost Dad in 2016, but at 86 we couldn't complain. My oldest nephew, my brother's boy will turn 21 this year, which amazes me, and now he is at agricultural college; it seems my agricultural college days are now two decades ago, how I don't know!

2018 was quite exciting as we bought a holiday cottage in Swanage and so have enjoyed lots of family fun there. **Melanie** caught the train to Banbury and cycled the rest to come and see us in the Autumn, which was great. **Lina** and I have been shooting together and also met up in Swanage. I feel very lucky to have a healthy family around me. I still work as a rural practice surveyor part-time to suit me, as well as running a campsite at Silverstone with the family, and now a holiday let to manage amongst lots of other things, so all in all very happy and busy as always. Hope to see some more of you before too long.

Caroline Walker For the last three and a half years, I have been running the child service, as a child and dolescent psychotherapist, for a charity that specialises in sexual abuse. I see children and young people, from three to twenty-five-years old, on a one-to-one therapeutic basis, and train and supervise therapists to work in this specialist area. I have been specialising in this trauma field for a while and use wonderful techniques to allow the trauma to pass through the body. I love the work, my clients and the people who work in the field. However, I have decided to take a break from this area of work temporarily to give my own body a rest for a while! So, I am in the process of setting up my own private practice now and I have also just started an equine facilitated psychotherapy course which will enable me to work with horses to help my human clients in a therapeutic manner.

I'm still based in Berkshire and still with my lovely partner, John, and I have also been fortunate enough to meet up with some of my old Westonbirt buddies this year including **Cordelia Gover (Harries), Coquita Mills (Marsh), Caroline Wilson (Pullin), Melanie Hobson, Claire Galer (Dorman)** and **Charlie Haynes (Hunt).**

Section 60 (1991)
Section Representative:
Rebecca Willows

No news returned this year

Section 59 (1990)
Section Representative:
Julia Roberts (Stubblefield)

No news returned this year

Section 58 (1989)
Section Representative:
Natasha McLeod (Marsh)

Natasha McLeod (Marsh) Life is very much governed by the school year and speeding by as a result. I'm working more hours for the parish which I enjoy although life becomes more like The Vicar of Dibley with each passing year.

Chantal Michelin (Lane) This year is one of change in many ways! Our children, Hector (16) and daughter Ines (13), both have important school exams in the summer: GCSEs and 13+ Common Entrance. Tim and I have a new member of the family, a Lurcher puppy called Willow, thanks to **Eleanor Findlater (Davies)** who found her for us. Willow is a very welcome addition to our home and my office!

Thankfully, despite the uncertainties of Brexit, my architectural practice Flower Michelin is busy. We have taken on two new team members and our work mainly focuses on private homes and development. We are now working all over the UK from Scotland to Somerset, and really enjoying the varied projects. My husband and I have also just finished our first development project in south west London which has been exciting.

I still see many Westonbirt girls and am in contact with 35+ plus ladies via a WB WhatsApp Group. Although we are scattered across the world, it makes it so easy to stay in touch!

Vanessa Newby I am an Assistant Professor at Leiden University in the Netherlands. I live with my Syrian partner in the Hague. All is good!

Melanie Rudland The past year has been a busy one, with two little children, a major house renovation and setting up a new company! The year has absolutely flown by, and to top it all, I got married in March. Exciting times! We are having another reunion in September and hope to see as many of our year there as possible.

Charlotte Turquet I have recently completed a training course to become a bereavement volunteer. I've already started seeing clients and I am really enjoying the work so far. In September my eldest child goes off to Newcastle University and my youngest leaves home for boarding school. I have enrolled on a four-year counselling course at a local college. Although the three children are now suitably house-trained and are up and off, I have young Wilbur to look after; a one-year-old cocker spaniel. He's pretty full on, but great fun.

Section 57 (1988)
Section Representative:
Fiona Stokes (Tobin) - (Section 45)

Amanda Spring was the only respondent for the section this year. She writes:

I am still living in Poland, close to Warsaw, and life is mainly taken up with business, dogs and horses. I'm not really sure that I have much news, and when I think about it I am not sure what I have been doing, but I know that I have been busy because time flies! I am still in the real estate business, and for now the market continues to be kind to us, although I guess we can expect some changes. I recently bought a new horse who I am loving. She suits me much better than the last one, who was super, but far too good for me; basically, I traded in the Ferrari for a nice safe little Volkswagen and this is a much better fit. I wish I had some exciting news, but sadly I think I have reached an age where I count a good crop of courgettes as noteworthy, so to avoid the risk of boring everyone to tears I will send my best wishes and sign off.

Section 56 (1987)
Section Representative:
Fiona Stokes (Tobin) - (Section 45)

Arabella Bishop I am still living in Dublin and about to celebrate my twenty years as Head of Sotheby's Ireland! I saw **Hetty Clark (Bowden)** during the year as she was in Dublin with her daughter Poppy, which was a treat.

Penny Cardwell (Samuel) I have been rather distracted recently as I dislocated and broke my ankle in three places at the end of January so have been trying to recuperate from that. What I have most definitely learnt is that injuries like that are so much harder to recover from as one gets older!

Anyway, my husband and I still live in Staffordshire, and I am still in the hotel business. I work for a hotel company part-time and I also have my own business which I set up with my business partner five years ago, offering revenue management consultation to small private independent hotels.

Hetty Clark (Bowden) Nothing much has changed! Still following four children around, the oldest now at university in Durham (following in his mother's footsteps). We're living in Gloucestershire and visiting Westonbirt almost daily for various sporting activities. Met up with **Bella Bishop** (Badminton) in Ireland this year. A real treat to catch up - so many wonderful Westonbirt memories! Could have talked all night.

Helen Curtis (Senior Stern) Unfortunately, Helen has broken her collarbone but managed to type the following: 'All good here, celebrating fifteen years at The Jolly Huntsman (Kington St Michael) this year.'

Juliet Davidson lives in London and mentioned in an email that she had climbed Mount Kenya in February. 'I'm still working in cricket (England Cricket Board) and expecting a busy summer with a Cricket World Cup over here (first time in twenty years) followed by an Ashes Series (against Australia - big contest for anyone involved in the cricket world).'

Sarah Harris-Burland (Pilling) I was recently promoted to Team Lead (at Royal Bank of Scotland in the Isle of Man) looking after staff access to systems. Natasha (daughter) has selected her GCSEs; I'm really impressed she decided to include Spanish in her options. Alexander (son) is off to high school in September. He is currently learning piano and clarinet (now plays in the IOM Youth Orchestra).

Vanessa Kearney (Richardson) A brief phone conversation with her husband Joe confirms they are living in Buckinghamshire and reveal they are both nurses doing shift work.

Annabel Kicks (Clothier) Annabel has disappeared from the Section contacts list but was apparently present at a year group gathering in November 2017, as was **Kate Auckland**.

Caitlin Limmer (Gardner) is still teaching running and putting on events for The Bearcat Running Club. Her son (17) is a drummer at The BRIT School in Croydon and daughter (15) is at school locally (home is in Isleworth).

Juliana Nash (Blanch) is working from home in Crudwell as a chiropractor and cranial-sacral therapist. Her daughters Elsa and Beth are thirteen and ten respectively and both enjoy skateboarding. Jules was divorced five years ago but is currently 'in a happy relationship with a lovely man who lives on a lake'. She keeps in touch with **Catherine Sutton, Kate Nutland** and **Hetty Clark.**

Sarah Rowntree (Jones) lives near Amersham. She sadly lost her father in April last year after a short illness. Her son Henry is fourteen and started at Harrow last September. She sees **Philippa Greey,** whose family was at the same prep school as Henry. She also periodically catches up with **Penny Cardwell (Samuel).**

Libby Warner (Glen) We're still living in Adelaide, South Australia where we've been for almost twelve years now. My husband is semi-retired and running a successful business, specialising in collectables. I have returned to teaching in secondary schools after a four-year break. I love it. Students today generally have a strong sense of morality, especially where racism, sexism and environmental issues are concerned. It's interesting as these issues reflect our future society.

Our fundraising in memory of our youngest daughter Sophie continues. She would have been 21 in 2017 which prompted us to reflect upon the importance of memories and time spent as families, so our donations go to Make-a-Wish Foundation.

Our eldest is engaged and planning a wedding. When did I become old enough for that to happen? Having qualified in Psychology, she is just finalising her masters in Social Work. We are incredibly proud of her commitment to supporting all members of communities. She is an incredible feminist and some of her objections to traditional wedding rituals etc. have prompted animated discussion.

My hip replacement became a security incident in Melbourne last year. I was stunned with the words 'Stand down, stand down. Artificial joint. Stand down.' My family thought a dumpy, middle aged, secondary school teacher, clearly having a bad hair day, and with a battered handbag, prompting a possible security alert, was highly amusing.

Our last UK visit was in 2014. I'm keen to visit again. British history takes some beating and there is so much just taken for granted including the history around Westonbirt. I'd like to explore that more.

Our three dogs keep us busy. We are downsizing within the next year and will be moving closer to the coast. I'm really looking forward to that.

Lara Webb was rushing out of her door in Hawkesbury Upton with at least one child when I phoned her. However, she gave me a new email address and a little online search reveals that she and two others set up TRIA Recruitment in 2015, specialising in IT and business transformation, based in Bristol.

Section 55 (1986)
Section Representative:
Emma Lack (Fitch)

No news returned this year

Sections 53 and 54 (1983-5)
Section Representative:
Sarah Clunie

Sarah Clunie reports that no news has been received from either section.

Sections 51 and 52 (1981 and 1982)
Section Representative:
Lizzie Mobbs (Overton)

No news returned this year

Section 50 (1980)
Section Representative:
Lou Walker (Foord)

No news returned this year

Section 49 (1979)
Section Representative:
Fiona Merritt

Funso Adegbola (Ige) My school, The Vale College, in Ibadan is celebrating its twenty-fifth anniversary this November. Any Westonbirt old girl in Nigeria anytime is welcome to visit; do get in touch.

My son got married to his heartthrob in December; they are enjoying their married life in Lagos.

I was looking at the photos I took with my cousin, **Morenike** in 2014, when we both went back to visit the School and attended Speech Day – we have good and happy memories of our time at Westonbirt and Dorchester House.

Mary Ashworth (Moriarty) Life is certainly very full. We currently have two gorgeous little grandchildren and another due in July - we are that old! Rob and I are both busy working for a church and a linked charity that have just opened a cafe in Camden where various related community projects take place. We had an amazing trip to Korea and Jeju last year for a family wedding and I recently had a great time in Norway, enjoying an unusual amount of snowfall. A big kid at heart!

Cheng Sim Chan Life is still, thank goodness, generally boring. I am still in Malaysia, still working in insurance, due to go to Singapore for the IPBA conference. I may 'ships passing in the night style' see **Katri Skala** in May/June when I come over for a flying visit for a friend's sixtieth.

Neelam Christie (Gunther) Fit and well and happy. I am still working in a GP practice as a 'chief dragon' (practice manager!) in order to fund my holiday habit! Skiing and sailing are always on the agenda with our first visit to Madeira later this year. Sadly, I have not made any Westonbirt reunions but would love to meet up with people.

Myfanwy Edwards (Lougher) Had a fabulous trip to Australia over Christmas and the New Year, going on to New Zealand where we caught up with **Joanna Kidson (Rowson)** and Phillip. It was lovely to see Jo after so many years and catch up with all the news.

This last year we have acquired another granddaughter, Megan, and I have set up the Cowbridge Food Collective - an online farmers market, allowing those who can't attend a Saturday morning market to purchase online, then collect on a Thursday evening from twenty different producers all from within thirty miles. No waste, no packaging and low food miles.

I'm still busy with the weekly Saturday farmers market and supplying cakes to four local tea rooms, plus the occasional special occasion cake. We've just started lambing on the farm so a busy five weeks ahead of us.

Alison Kerby (Wilson) My daughter, Georgie, is still working as a solicitor in London and still seems to be enjoying city life. My son Olly is starting at Sandhurst in May and my youngest, Fraser is still farming pedigree Shropshire and Poll Dorset sheep. Life is always very hectic with our surveying business and being assistant farmers (often to be found standing in a gap when the sheep need moving!); we have one eye on potential retirement (scary thought) but that's as far as it goes at the moment.

I did manage to return to Westonbirt last year for the ninetieth birthday garden party with my mother who hadn't been back since I left. It was lovely to have a tour of the school to see all of the changes that have been made. I was very sad to see that Holford House was no longer in existence. A great shame to lose that link to the original family but interesting to see the displays and archives in the old Holford dormitories.

Joanna Kidson (Rowson) We have now had a whole year of being 'kid free'. Jono (20 in July 2019) is now happily settled in Christchurch studying Engineering and kept busy by studies, sailing and UCM (University of Canterbury Motorsport). Bex (23 in November 2019) is now into her fifth year of studying; her initial BA with a double major in Geography and Sociology has morphed into a BA Hons in Sociology and a BSc in Geography.

Mid-2018, hubby Philip was pushed into early retirement via a work redundancy scheme. After a long 'holiday', we are considering a lot of options with working 9 to 5, five days a week being the least likely choice. Even with the empty nest, I seem to be busier than ever, and it may even be that I return to paid employ, leaving Philip at home with the chores. At the moment, I have a short-term contract to put systems in place in our church office; after the relief of filling the six-month office administrator vacancy, it was dashed by the post holder departing after seven weeks, meaning that something had to be done! Currently, I am being successful in declining a long-term appointment but only just!

It was great to catch up with **Myfanwy Edwards (Lougher)** when she and Richard came exploring New Zealand farm life earlier this year and travelled across country to spend the day with us in Taupo. The kids' rooms are available for guests – do come over.

Joan Lowton (Mullens) No major news although I had a new hip at the end of January and am really pleased with progress so far - walking pain free, back at work and hoping to get on the bike soon. I have, of course, been very good at doing my exercises! We had our fair share of trips last year to Malta, Luxembourg, Spain and a 'quick' trip to Australia for my nephew's wedding, which was lovely, and to Norway to see the Northern Lights, which I'm very happy to say came out to play! We're going to Canada in May and plan to go to Africa later in the year so I'm hoping to try out my new hip with some good walking.

Philippa Meikle (Main) All is well but nothing really to report, though.

Fiona Merritt I'm now a 'full' Aunty as Rex joined Lola last year for one half-brother, and the other one is expecting their first imminently. Also finding more out about executor duties – mainly for Mother but more just started for my cousin. Still 'plodding' (I was in the background for May's Royal Wedding) and diving, but Mother-related tasks took precedence with the unusual achievement of keeping one house in order all year (just not mine!) I did manage to join friends for a skiing week in Austria at the last minute and returned there again this year – blue skies & snow-capped mountain views a good restorative.

Mainly telephone catch-ups with **Marguerite Williams (Morris)** during her UK-wide trips but we did manage to co-ordinate dinner in July as she and Jock returned from Cornwall to fly back to California.

Marion Minton A tough few years at this time; I will update when there is good news.

Andrea Radman (Beattie) Still doing the yoga - not really making a living as yet but I enjoy it.

Nicola Tehel (Palmer) I am still in Devon (living on holiday), gazing out to sea at every opportunity (the main reason for moving) and am the local area assessor/coordinator for PAT.org, (Pets as Therapy). As part of social prescribing, I'm working with the local NHS hospitals to get the right dogs (and cats) and their owners visiting people on the hospital wards. This also extends into the community, to memory clinics, elderly care homes and schools. I can't give details but, boy! is what the visiting teams do valuable and rewarding.

This blends nicely alongside my therapy work under Nikki.Yoga (formerly WindsorYogaTherapy.com).

I'm zooming around in a pink Fiat 500, perfect for Devon lanes but being a Twin Air, it can get up the hills too!

Sally Scheffers Zombie impression just now as I am at the tail end of lambing and have very little help.

Marguerite Williams (Morris) We moved my mother, **Anne Morris** (staff) from Nutfield to an assisted-living complex in Cornwall last year where she is in the same complex as her brother; her niece, who lives nearby, has been a fantastic help. I have managed to get over a few times to see her. Jock and I are still living in California where I am working as an IT auditor generating SOC reports and ISO certification for cloud service providers. Fortunately, work is being really flexible about me making extended trips to the UK. We have our son David living with us, saving money on the excessive costs of renting in the Bay Area. Our daughter Helen is living in Edinburgh and currently taking a three-month sabbatical doing circus training.

Section 48 (1978)
Section Representative:
Amiel Price

We had a happy reunion lunch at Tetbury followed by an interesting historical tour of Westonbirt House with **Miss Challis**, our former Geography teacher. The current staff were laughing at me for still calling her Miss Challis - I can't bring myself to call her Diana, doesn't seem right! She showed us a huge panel of service bells that were discovered only a few years ago. They had been hidden behind a panel just above the door into 'Hades'. It was great to catch up with **Amelia Trevethick, Alicia Holmes (Rolston), Tella Wormington, Gillie Mccollum (Isaacs), Claire Staveley, Stephanie Wolfe (Binder), Charlotte Walpole, Carolyn Henson, Charlotte Harvey (Edgar), Liz White,** and **Jo Melhuish (Marchbank)**.

Sad news this year from our year group as we heard of the death of **Sarah Gustafson (Rehman)**. She was in Dorchester House and seemed always to be sharing a dorm with me. She left after 0 Levels and we lost touch although I know **Sara Jefcoate** from the year above had kept in contact with her.

Polly Davies Congratulations go to Polly whose multi-award-winning company Marco Polo Travel has just celebrated its thirty-year anniversary with its best trading months ever. She wrote 'I used my business background in marketing to set up Marco Polo Travel in January 1989, the first travel agency in the UK to specialise in walking and adventure holidays. We also provided seminars to encourage women to travel, "Getting Going and Staying Safe", for which people travelled from the USA and parts of Europe to attend. I gave lectures for Westonbirt girls each year to give them the confidence to consider more exciting gap year destinations. Galapagos, the Caucasus, Patagonia and Indochina have been popular destinations as well as luxury holidays to the Cote d'Azur and various parts of Central Europe by the Orient Express.'

Charlotte Harvey (Edgar) Many things remain unchanged in the Harvey household; Steve is still enjoying semi-retirement with a few consultancy jobs around to keep the grey cells in order, my projects continue: Barebones Theatre Project, Align for Learning special needs training course and the Life Stories intergenerational project.

William continues to enjoy Hong Kong and James is living and working in London in the fashion world but dreaming of warmer climes with his Australian girlfriend. Meanwhile Elinor is about to develop, direct and produce her next show for her company, Living Room Circus, and Isobel is applying to UCL for a PGCE in secondary art. So, the teaching gene is alive and kicking!

Our most exciting moment of last year was Elinor's beautiful wedding in a cow barn in Sussex - we now have a gorgeous daughter-in-law who is part of the circus team too!

Next year's plans are for an extended trip to America (Steve is hoping this will be on a motorbike - hmm!) and I shall be accompanying my mum to the Passion Plays in Oberammergau in September. No grandchildren yet so I expect now is the time to get away!

Really enjoyed catching up with the class of '78 at Westonbirt in September with a noisy lunch, a tour with Miss Challis and tea in the Library! I still meet up regularly with **Jo Melhuish (Marchbank)** and spent a great day at the Love Supreme Festival in July with **Zee Lunn (Marchington)**. So, all in all keeping busy.

Jane John (Thomas) Little changes! Just another year older!

Johanna Justice Not much to report in the last year, having to get a newer car is about as exciting as it gets here! Saw three days of England v India Cricket Test at Southampton to secure the series. Nail-biting stuff. Had various trips - to Beaulieu House and Motor Museum, Longleat Safari Park, including the house and also the Festival of Lights which was mind-blowing. If you have not been, it's worth it. Now I'm pottering along with wild and windy weather and hoping to go abroad in the Spring.

Susan Kennedy (Sheard) The last year has been busy with work embarking on a massive CRM project for the group I work for, Restore plc. I even had to hire a project manager as it's too much for me and my team to deal with.

I was proud to do the London Marathon last year with my eldest son, James, and the daughter of a friend who died three years ago. It was the hottest London marathon EVER and was quite hideous. We raised a lot of money for the Lords Taverners.

Gordon, my hubby, continues to produce loads of shows for Radio 4 and to do some acting; this year he is filming for the third series of 'Harlots' on ITV with a range of fantastic wigs. Luckily, he is on a break from filming as last Sunday he hit a lamppost at full pelt on his push bike and although the helmet took a lot of impact, his jaw was badly fractured and had to be put back together with 3 titanium plates.

James (26) is still working in data analytics for Lloyds Banking Group and Patrick (24) is loving his job in Toronto and is engaged to Mary Claire who he met at Bristol University and they get married on May 25th!

In six weeks' time, I will be running the Paris Marathon, my seventeenth marathon and fourth since having breast cancer. I am fundraising for Cancer Research for all the people we know who have cancer, have had cancer and have died of cancer. Far too many.

Had a great catch up with some Westonbirt friends last summer, Tella Wormington, Cally Henson, Fee Robertson, Gillie Mccollum (Isaacs), Angie Yorath (Haviland) and still see Rachel Dillon (Nobes) often.

Joanna Melhuish (Marchbank) I am so sad to hear of **Sarah Gustafson (Rehman)**. Really have no news this year.

Amiel Price Sadly my father died just after his 92nd birthday in July. It was rather sudden for us all and being the last parent, it marks the end of an era. It has left a larger than expected hole in our lives, although he was such a quiet and undemanding gentleman. I remember the laughs we had at one of the school fêtes when, at one of the stalls, he tried his hand at walking on upturned flower pots whilst holding an open umbrella and a handbell, which he was trying so hard not to ring as he wobbled across. It's like life, isn't it - trying to balance everything.

I had a useful distraction during the autumn with the self-publication of my book. It's a collection of love letters written to my Grandmother by Norman Wells during WW1. It includes his amusing cartoon drawings, extracts from both their diaries and many photographs, both from home and Egypt and Palestine. It's a fascinating insight into an era now gone and reveals a charming and poignant story as the couple's love for each other develops. It's called *From Handsworth to Hebron with the Herefords, 1917 Letters and Diary* and is available from me.

I'm getting a lot of pleasure from singing in a newly-formed choir called Mumbles a Cappella. We had a Christmas concert, and then an Easter one with the beautiful Miserere by Allegri, both sung in my local church. One lady said that we transformed the church into a cathedral with our singing, which is lovely praise. She may, however, find it a bit different if she comes to our Latin American concert this summer!

Lorraine Stanton (Martin) Having sold our farm in Wiltshire, Mark and I are now settled in Great Missenden, Buckinghamshire, and are firmly engaged in the experience of being grandparents. We have a large garden, which I'm looking forward to attending to, and lovely, welcoming neighbours, which has been a delight. I continue to cater for weddings and parties and have been rising to the challenge of an increasing number of vegan requests. The learning continues.

Stephanie Wolfe (Binder) It was great to meet up with some of the year back in September at Westonbirt and see some parts of the school I had never seen before.

Life is still busy. My husband Simon was seriously ill just before Christmas and then his department was closed, and he was made redundant in January, so we haven't had the best start to the year.

In an effort to boost our finances we have put our granny annexe up on Airbnb, moving the tortoises who were overwintering there into the ex-bedroom of Alex. I have been rebuilding their summer accommodation in the garden and am hoping it is more secure as they managed to escape last time and went missing all winter.

I am still doing lots of gardening, music and church stuff, though we now have a new part-time priest in charge so that helps.

Eldest daughter Rebecca is working in Athens with refugees, Flo is still a land agent in Lewes and running marathons, Alexander is still in PR in London and has a delightful boyfriend and Alan finally got a full-time contract with Shepherd Neame in marketing. He gets free samples and the occasional free tickets to cricket matches, so life isn't all bad!

Section 47 (1977)
Section Representative:
Fiona Leith

Katharine Hill (Cemlyn-Jones) This has been a year of highs and lows. My wonderful father died on Christmas Day 2017 aged 100, my mother-in-law the following October and my brother-in-law (my sister's husband) just a few weeks later, of the fast-acting degenerative brain disease CJD. The promise of new life brings hope in dark times and we are excited that we are to be first-time grandparents this year as our daughter and her husband, and also our son and his wife, are both expecting babies this year. I continue to enjoy my role as UK director of the charity Care for the Family which aims to strengthen family life across the nation. I have written a few books and the latest, *Left to Their Own Devices – confident parenting in a world of screens*, has given me increasing opportunities to write and speak for the national media. I am still in touch with **Leigh Ralphs (Davidson)** and had the privilege of writing the foreword for Old Westonbirtian **Anita Cleverly's (Dodds)** book, and of seeing her and her sister **Miranda** at the launch in Oxford.

Cherry James (Lucas) Very briefly, as I am leaving for Heathrow in an hour's time to attend the wedding of the daughter of **Sharon Chen** in Sydney. Still working at London South Bank University lecturing in Law, very pleased to say that my book, based on my PhD thesis, was published in January (*Citizenship, Nation-Building and Identity in the EU: The Contribution of Erasmus Student Mobility*). Freddie lives in Basel and works as an organist in a lovely church there, and freelances as an organist and harpsichordist, mostly in Switzerland and Germany. Anna is a chartered surveyor working in London, living about a mile away from us, so we see her often which is great. I'm in touch with **Sharon** (obviously!) and with **Corinna Kershaw (Chown)** and **Henrietta Ewart** (we enjoy meeting for Indian meals when we can). I also had the great pleasure of seeing **Nicky Vollkommer (Sperry)** in December as Freddie again played the organ for her wonderful English-style carol services in south west Germany.

Serena Jones (Walthall) We now have four adults living in the house, each with their own agenda and no sign of us empty-nesting just yet. One daughter was in New Zealand last year and Dave and I did finally get over there for a holiday, just before she came back.

Still doing choir, woodwork, bridge, RDA, Guide Dogs and Westonbirt Association stuff but also a large amount of time in our woods in Herefordshire. We did some serious 'thinning' of mature trees a year ago and have planted nearly a thousand replacements in the lovely dry weather of Jan/Feb, mostly planted by Dave, with me doing the layout of what should be planted where. The young shoots are already being eaten by deer, so we are now busy putting guards round the most precious trees and eating as much venison as we can.

About to catch up with **Mary Wickenden**, who is calling in next week. She has recently moved from London to East Sussex.

Ruby Lau Ruby found time in her busy schedule to send a brief update: I have been in Sydney for two weeks running a course which just ended on Friday, and I flew out that very evening for Malaysia, where I am for a few days before going to Chennai, where I have been a consultant with an AMI teacher training institute, mentoring schools and teachers. It gives me the opportunity to travel back to see my mum in Kuala Lumpur nearly every month. She is now almost ninety-one!

Recently, I haven't been able to schedule my travels to be in the UK during reunion and event dates, but I hope to one of these days. Would love to see everyone and catch up with their news.

Fiona Leith (Goodbody) Firstly, thank you so much to everyone who replies to my Westonbirt Association News begging letter each year. It is so nice to hear from you all, and it would be great to hear from some others too!

We had a busy year in 2018, with the entire summer arranged round four weddings. A nephew and a niece in Scotland, and friends in Hampshire and California - what a good excuse for a holiday that last one was! We returned to places I last visited thirty-eight years ago. Surprisingly, the Grand Canyon hadn't changed (although the facilities were much nicer). Las Vegas was as awful as I remember. Generally, the food had improved. Last month saw a terrific holiday with my sisters **Susie Younger (Goodbody)** and **Seonaid Coreth (Goodbody)** and their husbands to Oman. We had an amazing trip, with a pair of very wild drivers guiding us round the country.

I heard briefly from **Fiona Dix (Bolus)** to say that she is a bit tied up with puppies just now.

Tina Panton (Galanis) Things are looking up. Fawlty Towers aka Villa Galanis finally opened to the public mid-August and I think it's going to provide a bit of income, which will be good. Hard work but worthwhile. You can find us on booking.com - but if you want to come and stay, email me and we can save their commission! Mates' rates! (You can contact her through her Section Rep or the school). Equally, if not more importantly, our HMRC nightmare has finally come to an end after five years. The relief is.... well, now we can get on with our lives again. Kids are fine, dogs and cats are fine, no news is good news! Love to you all.

Kathy Pratt Just over two years after retiring early I have managed to purchase a lovely, very quirky, cottage down in Devon, just up the lane from my partner. Plan A had been to redevelop part of my partner's Grade II Listed property, but this was not permitted so reluctantly I decided to buy my own place. It's actually turned out far better as I've got my own space, a delightful home and garden, it's even got sea views! It's given me a whole new lease of life; I feel as if I've only just retired!

It's over thirty years since I moved house so I was delighted to get a buyer for my old home in Kent who really appreciated it as it is. As a surveyor he didn't give me any hassle and we completed within three months, what a relief.

The last couple of years have been a nightmare with losing Mum, then within nine months, my fiercely independent Dad experiencing a major life-changing event.

I very nearly missed the chance to buy my dream home when Dad's live-in carer had to drop everything to fly back to Poland because of a burst water pipe in her flat. We'd about twenty-four hours to put a whole team in place to cover thirty-six hours so I could leave Dad to view the property.

The house was being sold privately and I'd been waiting six months to see it; I was scheduled as the first viewing, with someone else scheduled for later the same day. I made an offer which was accepted, we shook hands on it, and were all so pleased we ended up hugging each other! The rest is history.

Leigh Ralphs (Davidson) The School's ninetieth birthday in May 2018 was great fun. We held the Association's Reunion Day as part of their annual Picnic in the Park event, and it worked really well, especially as the sun was shining. The night before Guyon and I had joined **Karen Broomhead (Fielding)** and **Jenifer Greenwood** amongst others at the 90th Ball held in the Library and Great Hall, which brought back fond memories of our Leavers' Ball in October 1976 when I first met my husband on a blind date, organised by **Fiona Dix (Bolus)**!

Our highlight of last year was spending October/November driving around New Zealand, staying mostly in B&Bs/Lodges. We began our 'Senior' sixtieth birthdays' adventure in Auckland on the North Island, going further north to the gorgeous Bay of Islands to start and then zig-zagging our way down to the South Island, ending up in Queenstown for a few days (no bungee jumping for us though!) before reluctantly heading home.

It is a stunning country with spectacular scenery every minute of the journey - from magnificent surf and sand dunes to postcard-perfect beaches with turquoise waters, volcanic mud pools and geysers, mammoth national parks with wonderful walks and smouldering volcanoes, beautiful lakes and glaciers, incredible waterfalls and the sublime Fiordlands. We travelled mainly by car but also enjoyed being on the water in small boats when we could, crossing the Marlborough Sounds on the Inter-Island ferry and travelling on the TranzAlpine railway (one of the 'world's most scenic train journeys') from Christchurch (still not rebuilt after the earthquakes) to Greymouth (gold mining country). We managed to break up the driving with lots of walks (or 'tramps' as the Kiwis call them) which usually ended up at a lake or a waterfall etc.

We also enjoyed learning about the indigenous Maori culture, visiting the Waitangi Treaty Grounds, where we experienced a Haka (think All Blacks), followed by a twilight walk with members of the local Maori tribe in the Waipoua Forest to see the Kauri trees, one of which is estimated to be over 3000 years old.

Highlights are very difficult to point out as everywhere was stunning in its own way, but we loved our overnight boat trip (for just ten people) on Doubtful Sound (more inaccessible and remote than Milford Sound so we were the only boat there - it's known as the 'place of silence') where I caught the biggest fish of the day (a New Zealand blue cod!) It's one of NZ's largest fiords and as we glided through a maze of forested valleys carved by glaciers, saw masses of waterfalls, Fiordland penguins, seals and a pod of dolphins – awesome!!

Penny Sloman (Sheard) Horry continues to live in Saudi Arabia working for Aramco so I visit regularly including trips to Lebanon, Emirates and Bahrain and Jordan.

The boys are still scattered from Australia to America to London, so I have to travel to see them too.

Tennis continues to be the biggest source of joy in my life with bridge exercising my brain.

Mummy died last year, which was very sudden and sad, but she was not in good health despite her spirit.

I have begun volunteering at Wandsworth prison as a mentor which is hopefully a useful tool to the prisoners.

Nicola Vollkommer (Sperry) A busy year, with highlights and lowlights alternating with each other. Two more grandchildren to look forward to - nothing beats that for joy and gratitude! Our Reutlingen Festival of Carols is becoming part of the local culture, with the Reutlingen and Dettingen Cathedrals filled to capacity this past December. What a delight to have **Cherry,** Simon and Anna James there to hear Freddie play! The best possible Christmas treat imaginable. Joy was followed by tears, as my beloved Dad's health began to fail, and he finally slipped away at the end of January. He had lived a full and blessed life, but the loss leaves us devastated and coping with a world which feels forlorn and drab without him. His memorial service was a testimony to the impact he had on the lives of so many people.

Other news? I continue with my speaking and book tours, meeting a lot of interesting people, surprised and grateful that my books are being so well received. Church is doing well; we're enlarging the building, Helmut is gradually handing over responsibility to the young generation, and we're grateful for flourishing youth work and many wonderful volunteers!

Jenny Webb (Binder) I don't have very much news to share this year. I am bumbling along doing my usual stuff; 'governing' at two schools, tennis, bridge, singing, spending time looking after members of the family. Our saddest news was having to say goodbye to our fifteen-year-old Beagle Tully. Never having been a dog person it took me by surprise how devastated I was to lose him. Dogs interpose themselves into your daily life in a way that cats don't… although I am devoted to them!

We had a nice break last October at a family friend's daughter's wedding on Martha's Vineyard. Lovely warm weather and a great party. Then John and I headed up to the north of New England to see the Fall colours. Temperatures were a little different and we even had some snow! All very beautiful and we also saw Niagara Falls, so that is two of the world's great waterfalls seen - now we have to travel to South America to tick off the third! I love seeing **Leigh Ralphs (Davidson)**, **Serena Jones (Walthall)** and others involved with the Westonbirt Association even though the three-hour drive can be a little tedious. Hope to see many more friends at the Association Day, it really is good fun!

Mary Wickenden Hi folks, I am writing this update from Kampala in Uganda where I go with almost monotonous regularity these days (for short work trips)! This is because I have made a big transition in the last six months and am now working at the Institute of Development Studies, part of the University of Sussex, down near sunny Brighton. The job is similar to my previous one at UCL, doing research about disability in a number of low-income countries in Africa and Asia. However, I now have more of a leadership role, so it's a steep learning curve, and so far, going well, but with rather hectic amounts of overseas travel!

On the home front, I have also moved out of London down to Lewes, a lovely old town that I am sure some of you know. I've bought a house very near the centre with beautiful hilly views in all directions. I am enjoying being able to walk everywhere and taking some hearty leisure walks. Just getting to know people and will be doing things like sailing and swimming in the sea that I love. Do come and visit if you are nearby!

Section 46 (1976)
Section Representative:
Jean Stone

Nicola Capewell (Wilson) very kindly sent me the piece below about the ninetieth birthday reunion:

'Prosecco and nibbles in one of our rooms at the Cirencester Premier Inn provided us with an excellent start to what proved to be a most enjoyable weekend in Gloucestershire. Vaguely reminding us of illicit midnight feasts decades before, **Jean Stone (Borritt), Alix Gibson** and I convened to reminisce and to plan for the following day's events at Westonbirt. Jean and I would go to the church service while Alix marshalled the picnic etc. We then agreed a place to rendezvous.

Meeting up in the grounds on that warmish Saturday in May, it was good to see so many others participate in the day's events. Serenaded by the choir, with pop-up shops selling memorabilia (I am the proud owner of the ninetieth anniversary book and another mug, as well as being several quid lighter) and food outlets aplenty, no wonder we were having a good time!

And that good time was considerably enhanced by meeting up with others from our time at Westonbirt: **Maggie Metcalfe (Haviland), Susan Johnston (Edwards) aka Spud** and **Gill Marriott (Gillett)** from our year and **Betzan Mar (Wing)** from the year above. Along with Maggie's husband Jeremy, we pooled our lunch provisions, then strolled around the grounds and viewed the exhibition detailing the history of the school. Memories flooded back (mostly good, but some not so good) aided no doubt by a visit to Hades and the shock of the staff room no longer being the staff room...

For the finale of the day we opted to return to church for a good old hymn singing session. Sadly, Miss Naylor and Mr Higgins were no longer with us, having their regular spat over which verse we were supposed to be practicing, but we appreciated the opportunity to immerse ourselves once more in what was another Westonbirt tradition.

Times move on though and rightly so. Whatever else may have changed by the time Westonbirt celebrates its centenary, the view of the main house from the driveway and the ethos of the school will surely have stayed the same.'

Susan Hopkins (Heather) Following the passing of my mother in September 2017 after a short but difficult period, I decided it was time to retire from my position at Milton Keynes College and move back to the Cotswolds; this we did in February 2018. We sold our property in Buckinghamshire and moved to my mother's house in preparation for selling the property as Roger and I had often spoken of retiring to Somerset to live nearer our daughter.

In December 2018 we did just that and moved in to a property next door to Becca and Chris. Eight days later Becca gave birth to our first grandchild, Pippa! We have some renovating to do to our property this year and hope to be all straight by the end of the summer. So far Somerset is fab.

Sally Richards (Stevenson) Sally apologised for the late reply to my request for news. Unfortunately, she had fallen in the street and broken her arm and dislocated her elbow, necessitating surgery to pin and plate. Although she is on the mend, Sally is frustrated that she cannot drive at present; as Sally lives in the remotest part of Pembrokeshire this is a real inconvenience. We wish her a speedy recovery.

She writes: 'The main things of note are that I lost my lovely dad in October, and that we managed to move into our newest barn conversion just in time for Christmas. Also, that I enjoyed meeting up with **Mary Ross** and **Nicky Capewell** in September, and that I was really pleased to see **Jean** at Dad's funeral, albeit on a sad occasion.

I also hear from **Jane Baker (Vass)** and **Sue Johnston (Edwards)**, and was chatting to **Cherry Stratford (Perkins)** in the summer as we both live in Pembrokeshire and found out that we had a Westonbirt connection!'

Clare Savoca I celebrated my sixtieth in style, renting a hall and having fun with about forty of my friends. Unbeknown to me they had prepared two videos for me. One from my family in the States and one from my friends around the world. I found out that I was part Jewish, so I started learning Hebrew. I also retired early so am now 'a lady of leisure'.

Jean Stone (Borritt) It has been a busy first year of retirement but one which I have thoroughly enjoyed. It has given me the opportunity to try lots of new things including willow weaving, printing my own fabric and making Christmas decorations, a lampshade and cushion cover, the last two of which I am ridiculously proud. The willow weaving was less successful – my sweet pea trellis cone had a definite tilt to one side.

My holiday to Scotland to learn sea kayaking was wonderful. The scenery was so beautiful, and we were lucky enough to see an otter, eagles, wild deer, dolphin and seals. We also saw beautiful starfish and sea urchins beneath us as we paddled around the edges of Loch Torridon and Kishorn. We had one wild weather day spent inland on Loch Maree. It was very choppy, but thanks to my trusty sea-sickness pills I was able to enjoy the exhilarating experience.

A second week was spent on a National Trust working holiday. I went to Wasdale and Eskdale and spent my week clearing non- native small trees from the Hardknott forest, then replanting the same area with oak saplings. Some time was spent learning the basics of dry-stone walling as well as clearing overgrown footpaths and removing bracken from an archaeological site overlooking Ulverston and Morecambe Bay. It was hard work but good fun, so I have signed up for a Carmarthenshire coastal holiday in May.

I had an almost unbelievable weekend in November, when in the space of three days my youngest daughter announced her first pregnancy, my eldest became engaged, my brother set his wedding date and his daughter, my eldest niece, also became engaged. I have just attended the first of eight weddings in the next two years and am very excited about the arrival of grandchild number one in June.

Nicky Capewell (Wilson) and I continue to meet regularly for lunchtime organ concerts in Birmingham. I have also seen **Sally Stevenson** and **Tanya Sperry**. Sadly, both have lost their dads in the past few months.

The Midland Art Centre (MAC) has accepted me as a volunteer and I am now part of the A team that has had extra training to help disabled members of the community access the various events that are held there. It is interesting work which I can do as and when able.

Section 45 (1975)
Section Representative:
Susie Younger (Goodbody)

Teresa Mockridge (Wormington) Disappointingly, my life is not the globe-trotting, award-winning career that I'm sure you all expected of me (not, as they say), and I don't really have any news except that I am still working and running, and would love to host a get-together here at our house in the school grounds, whilst we still have it, if anyone would like to come.

Jane Seymour Still happily living in Norfolk with Gordon and two border collies, still a wine merchant although travelling much less, sadly. We now have four grandchildren! Henry (2), Elspeth (2), Adam (six months), Charlie (two months); have managed to avoid nappies totally, thank goodness. I see/speak with **Clare Williams** often and am still in touch with **Lorna Hooley** and **Fiona Stokes**.

Fiona Stokes (Tobin) Main news on the domestic front is we had an interior wall removed last year to create a new kitchen. Still have twin sons living at home, both in employment, who have been inspired to cook their own meals, and the extra space is a delight.

Had a fun evening in February, with **Ali Cheeseman (Dorey)** and **Caroline Mant (Liddiard)** at Liddy's house, with our respective husbands. The ladies were still talking long after their menfolk had gone to bed! Looking forward to Glyndebourne with **Clare Williams** again this year. I keep in touch with **Lizzie Bennett (Phelps)** and **Trudy Evans (Wardle)** though sadly have seen almost nothing of **Anne Millman** since her husband has been so ill this past year.

I broke my left collarbone last May so arrived at Westonbirt with arm in sling and hubby driving me to the reunion. It was such fun to meet **Bettzan Mar (Wing)**, over from California, **Wendy Court (Williams) Vivienne Benson (Cottam)** and **Katrina Foster (Tolson)** that day.

Elinor Tolfree I'm still doing some instrumental teaching as well as some music therapy. I'm a volunteer for the two main musical charities, visiting musicians in need and helping them sort out applications for financial support. I'm currently doing a counselling course which I hope will take me to the next stage in life! I find there is always something to learn.

I have now been living in Dorset for just over thirty years which seems an amazing amount of time. I so love being here in an old house with a walled garden. The house is full of instruments and people playing music. I have a garden shed full of Indonesian instruments which come out onto the lawn in the summer in order to be played by a group of people and the same instruments travel to special schools for creative music work. I'd love to meet up with some other people from my time at Westonbirt.

Clare Williams Still working at Canary Wharf for Barclays. Finally moved into my house post extensive refurbishment in May but am now contemplating an extension. Must be mad. My dad is now ninety-three and has just moved into a dementia care home in Hindhead - he seems very happy and well cared for. Fortunately, he still recognises me and Hugh and our aunt, but struggles with friends he's known for seventy years. To keep my brain going I took to the boards in October and was very grateful that **Fiona Stokes** and **Lizzie Bennett** came along to support - I'm not inflicting any more acting on my fans for a while yet though! Still very grateful to Mrs Webb for everything she taught me about acting all those years ago.

Susie Younger (Goodbody) I am still trying to get our holiday house completed on the west coast of Scotland ready for letting out to tourists. I have no excuses now as the builders have finished so it is all down to my DIY skills, which is rather stressful.

We launched our small power boat last year and put it on a mooring in front of the house and have done a few courses as we have only done sailing before. It is rather exciting, and I am enjoying speeding around with the 300hp outboard!

We have just had a fantastic holiday in Oman, which is an incredible country and well worth a visit for its spectacular scenery and lovely people.

Our middle son got married here last August and we had to landscape a flat area for a marquee as we are on a hill and never thought with three sons that we would be hosting a wedding. We spent the whole summer watering, but it all looked good and the wedding went very well, thank goodness.

Section 44 (1974)
Section Representative:
Elizabeth Battye (Jones)

Elizabeth Battye (Jones) Our main family news this year is that our daughter gave birth to our first grandchild last November. They live about an hour away so not too far to visit. Our son is getting married in September. Fortunately, he has just moved to a new house within our village so it is lovely to have him so close.

Jennifer Denholm (Goodbody) I've had a rather exciting year. I now have three grandchildren and another one due very shortly. I have also bought a new house but can't move in until I've converted downstairs rooms into a bedroom and bathroom! Can't wait...

Pauline Jackson (Garrett) I am spending more time out at my home in Spain now that my eldest, Stephen, has moved there with his family. I have just returned from two weeks in India around the Golden Triangle, incorporating a few days volunteering at the Wildlife SOS sanctuary, working with elephants and sloth bears.

I then spent two weeks in Sri Lanka, with son Paul, followed by a solo trip to Nepal. My daughter, Laura, has just bought her first flat in Chiswick with her New Zealand partner; they both work in the film industry. My youngest son, David, lives with me in Weston along with his North American Akita, who gave birth to eight puppies just before Christmas, so much hard work! I see **Felicia Milocevic (Leman)** on occasion and play scrabble with **Charlotte England (Wren)** online, on a daily basis!

Caroline Lloyd (Pelham-Lane) Now I have passed 60 I felt that I could start pleasing myself a bit more and have semi-retired. I now work three days a week, still as a principal valuer at the Valuation Office, advising government clients on their property, largely the NHS. The nice thing is that I am now concentrating on interesting cases and teaching the bright young things, and some not so young! No more writing management reports, which I always hated and was really not very good at!

With my two extra days a week I am embarking on Project De-Clutter (greatly needed) at home, doing two aqua-aerobic sessions a week (doing me good and to my surprise quite fun!) and more sewing (tapestry) and reading which are pleasures I have greatly missed in recent years. I plan to start singing and piano again: last played aged fifteen in the practice rooms over the stables courtyard classrooms at Westonbirt. So that will be from scratch again, I think!

The family (now rather smaller following the deaths of Mother and Mother-In-Law) are well; Julian continues dealing with his court cases (sometimes harrowing) re welfare of children, and our son Guy is in his last year reading history at Aberystwyth. He plans to do a Teaching English as a Foreign Language course in the interim as an 'earner' whilst continuing serving as a reservist with the Royal Welsh (Fusiliers). Don't know if that is his future direction; we shall see!

Margaret Miller Brown I left Westonbirt in 1973 after my father finished his studies at Cambridge, and returned to California to complete high school and attend Stanford University where I studied Applied Earth Science. After a brief stint of living in Hawaii, hanging out on the beach in the morning and working in a cheesecake bakery in the afternoon, I decided to face reality and get my law degree. For many years, I lived and practiced in Colorado and New Mexico, specializing in natural resources law. My favourite job was representing the National Parks in the southwestern US and all the opportunities for travel that that afforded. I married an applied mathematician (who's also a very good cook) and we have two sons in their 20s, still in school, one of whom advocates on behalf of the disabled while the other hopes to pursue a career in neural engineering. I've been retired for some time and we now live in Berkeley, California, where I'm slowly remodelling a house and updating the garden.

I'm on Facebook as Margaret Miller Brown if anyone would like to connect.

Carol Pusey (Cleal) Continuing to enjoy music and sport in equal measure, filling time with viol playing, piano teaching and singing in a variety of small choirs, and running, swimming and cycling... all for fun!

Competing in a rather hilly 10k run in Alresford in June, in the hope of raising money for Cancer Research.

Very much enjoyed meeting **Valerie Byrom Taylor** from time to time in the past year, occasionally at concerts, but also at Val's beautiful home, to chat and enjoy her wonderful cooking!

Section 43 (1973)
Section Representative:
Sarah Thomas (Leslie)

Tish Golding Two years on from leaving work I am only just getting used to being so free. I have spent much of the time catching up on things I always wanted to do but hitherto hadn't had the time or energy for. So, I have started learning the piano! I couldn't read music or play a note, but I am now learning my first Grade One pieces. I find it incredibly hard, but I think it must be good for the brain. I'm also having singing lessons. I never dared to sing alone before, but I am gradually getting there. I love both the piano and singing and wish I had learnt at school! I've also joined Streatham Choral, a lovely, energetic and very friendly choir. We've sung some great pieces over the last two years. I'm looking forward to our Mozart concert at the end of March.

The other thing we wanted to do when we stopped work was travel. We had to delay travel plans for several months because of family illness but happily we're up and running and off to India, Kerala and Tamil Nadu, at the end of February. In April we are visiting **Zoe Littleton** at their place in Arles, and in June we are going to Sicily with **Anti Seymour Williams** and her husband. So, looking forward to all our planned travels.

Family-wise, our older daughter Maddie had a fourth baby, Pippa, last September. She has two other girls and a boy who is nearly ten. We see them often which is lovely. Harry is still temping and Louisa graduates from Hull University this year. She's doing drama. Maurice, my husband, spends most of the time in the garden but has also taken up painting. We decided we needed new hobbies to stretch ourselves but now we're used to retirement and have had some time off, we both plan to do some volunteering as well. My mum is eighty-eight now, still living independently in Selsey. I see her as often as possible.

This year I've seen **Zoe Littleton**, **Anti Seymour-Williams** and **Carol Brook (Kynnersley)** and had a weekend in Cheltenham with **Renee Dixon (Gunn)** and **Izy Williamson (Riddell)**. Hoping to see **Rekha Dutt (Ghose)** and **Sarah Thomas (Leslie)** soon.

(A big thank you to Tish for sending in the above news.)

Sarah Thomas (Leslie) I myself am still enjoying my job as Financial Controller of a Japanese company, currently in Coventry but soon to move to a newly-built premises in Warwick, which, luckily, is much closer to my home. We are looking forward to our oldest daughter's wedding in Rhodes in July. Still bell-ringing as much as I can in my spare time. My sister **Jean Leslie** (Section 41) still lives in Australia and is retired now. She will be visiting for a few months later in the year.

Section 42 (1972)
Section Representative:
Miranda Purves (Saxby-Soffe)

Libby Coats (Clover) and her husband are being the predictable loving grandparents. After losing their Labrador last year they have bravely taken on a new puppy so are enjoying the resulting chaos. They have also kindly given hospitality to my cousin who has recently moved to very near them.

Sally Gesua (Clifford) says that life continues at a fairly rapid pace with sport/bridge/grandchildren and holidays (not necessarily in that order!) So far this year they have travelled to Oman and Wales, were about to go skiing followed by a trip to Scotland, then a month in Menorca, golf in Prague and then Mauritius for a couple of weeks. Somehow, they are hoping to find the time to fit in a couple more trips too. Life seems good for her and she is managing to stay reasonably healthy, which is great news!

Diana Graham (Gantlett) sent in an immediate, if brief, response from Australia to my news request, saying that they were waiting for rain and then hoping to come over to England. (Diana had given me **Lulu Gordon-Canning's** contact details last year prior to my trip to Bhutan so that was most useful.)

Miranda Purves (Saxby-Soffe) I have just returned from a wonderful trip to Jordan and Israel where we saw lots of historical sites. The Biblical sites in Israel were somewhat crowded and full of jostling which was rather off-putting. It was very good to see **Guilia** and her brother who came to my mother's funeral last summer. Both our mothers had been at Downe House as schoolgirls, then jointly decided to send us to Westonbirt instead. It was only at Guilia's mother's funeral that my mother learned that they had both also worked at Bletchley Park during the war but had never discovered or discussed that.

Guilia Rhodes (Bartrum) has been too modest to mention this but has been lauded in the press for putting on the 'Edvard Munch: Love and Angst' exhibition at the British Museum which has been gaining excellent reviews.

Section 41 (1971)
Section Representative:
Jennifer Cope

June Barrow Green I'm still at the Open University as Professor of History of Mathematics and still rushing around the country and abroad giving talks about my research, mostly on mathematics developed in the First World War, the history of women in mathematics and nineteenth-century geometric models. On the sporting front, I have been doing quite a lot of cross-country running, and this year have the London and Berlin marathons to look forward to as well as the London Ride 100 cycle event. I am still in Islington but now have a table-tennis table in the garden, which is much in use when my partner, Reinhard, visits from Norway. I regularly see **Melisse Twist (Beanland)** and **Shan Rigby (Jones)**, and of course my sister **Belinda Trimble** who is in Somerset, close to where we grew up. My aunt **Dheidre Philips (Hornsby)** was 100 on 23 December last year and my cousins produced a wonderful album of her life including several pictures of her in various teams at Westonbirt. I am happy to report that at her birthday tea-party she was much more interested in the champagne and cake than she was in the sandwiches!

Jodie Buckley (Stephenson) After eleven years in the Isle of Man, (and after nearly twenty-five years in Yorkshire!) we decided to move back to the UK and found a beautiful spot on the Solway coast in southern Scotland. The house will be re-built in a modern style and enjoys views down to the Solway Firth. Our family (Scoto-philes all) live in Edinburgh and we visit them regularly. Ed has retired and has now been officially drafted onto the garden team, when not overseeing the design and build project. I have put watercolour painting on hold for a while but have plenty of ideas for when we settle down. Great to see **Kar (Fielding)** and Tony Broomhead, and last autumn we managed to rendezvous in Portugal, just to see if we could do it! I also joined her on one of the early garden tours of Highgrove, which is amazing, by any standards! Although we won't be able to properly host anyone anytime soon, it would still be fun to hear from anyone daring the frozen north! If you've missed it, Dumfries and Galloway is a charming county, with gently rolling hills, beautiful coastline, and feels less busy than other famous Scottish counties: (turn left after Carlisle).

Nicola Currie (Penley) I'm enjoying semi-retirement having reached my goal of 'weekends' which last longer than the working week (I am an agricultural apprenticeship ambassador for my local college). I have also taken on a voluntary fundraising role for our Grade I listed church so I'm learning a lot about writing grant applications and the Heritage Lottery Fund as well as church bells!

I hear from **Angela Neuhaus (Low)** who is in the Netherlands, where her husband is the Australian ambassador, and **Jane Wrobel (Wakefield)** who is still in the Lake District.

Diana Farrington (Broughton) I can't remember if I replied last year! If so, you will have heard that both my boys are now married and living back in Somerset on the farm, taking over its management as well as being involved in other techy engineering development. We are proud grandparents to little Lettie, born to Charlie and Millie in the blizzard of the Beast from the East, on the first day of spring last March.

On another snowy day in March it was lovely to catch up with so many of the Briggs and Grundy families at my godchild Ruth's very special wedding at Sandhurst.

Last April we enjoyed meeting Karen and Tony in Portugal and again soon after at the wonderful weekend of celebrations at Westonbirt, for the ninetieth birthday of the school and one hundred and fiftieth anniversary of the house. Westonbirt looked amazing. Having just returned from wonderful Seville and Granada I was completely awestruck by the beautiful surroundings of classical interior design and landscape which we were so privileged to enjoy, without realising, at school.

Shan Oakes (Jones) We are living in Knaresborough now to be near sons and families. My mum **Margaret (Mrs Jon**es who taught Domestic Science in the sixties) died aged eighty-eight in December 2017 in Harrogate Hospice after being a very keen grand/great-grandmother. She was coming to live with us, but her health decline overtook our plans. It was good to find her included in some of the photos displayed at the Westonbirt ninetieth birthday event, in one looking conspiratorial with French teacher Lynette Hunter (who I bumped into fourteen years ago in Uganda!) Bill Rigby and I are continuing to campaign on green issues e.g. fracking, air quality, pesticides, bees, swifts, marine destruction etc. Also, organising a new Knaresborough Festival to celebrate this lovely town. We should love to see anyone who would like to drop in if they are in our vicinity - please don't hesitate to get in touch. (You can contact her through her section rep or the school).

Section 40 (1970)
Section Representative:
Jennifer Cope

Jennifer Cope (Wells) We start lambing next week but with a much smaller flock than in previous years. I sing with a couple of local choirs and am Secretary to a Guild of Weavers, Spinners and Dyers. In addition, I also teach people to spin wool. **Karen Broomhead (Fielding)** and I went to see the Glyndebourne Touring Company in Norwich.

Clare Keep (Morton) I am still riding since last news submission. Ventured on two pony-trekking trips with friends and familiar ponies, first to Exmoor and then rode the Radnor Loop in the Brecon Beacons. Both totally different, hard work but enjoyable. The younger pals look after the older riders! Also competed at a dressage event for the first time; nerveracking but I can tick that off my to do list now. Time flies and retirement for me really is centred round the grandchildren and family.

Annabel Kerr (Johnston) In May I went with **Di Gale (Forwood)** to Westonbirt's ninetieth birthday celebration. So much change! Holford dorms completely restored to how they used to be in Lord Holford's day. A lot of reminiscing and lovely to walk round the grounds again. My fifth grandchild arrived in September. My days are full looking after three of them with help from Di who lives just around the corner from me.

Barbara Matthews (Powell) We are off to Vietnam and Cambodia tomorrow for three weeks; it should be such an interesting holiday with lots of really fascinating places and experiences lined up. We had lots of lovely holidays last year, and a month in Austria and Slovenia in September. Luckily, we are keeping pretty well and active and able to enjoy retirement.

Caroline Sanders I have some exciting news! Having been single all these years I am to be married to a wonderful man called Douglas Cole on 31st August this year. We will be married at our village church in Datchet with a reception at Dorney Lake Rowing Centre. All our families and friends will be with us, so it promises to be a wedding with a lot of guests. Another big event this year is my sister Daphne's seventieth birthday, another great family celebration.

Tizzie Short (Harbottle) After years as an opera singer I retrained and gained a university degree seven years ago, in Integrative Counselling and

Psychotherapy. With my private practice in south west London I see individuals and couples and encourage clients to sing and breathe, (very dear to my heart!) while listening to and supporting them. I still sing when asked... funerals most recently!

My great-niece and her three brothers have all been at Westonbirt... two of the boys are still there, and I now have a small granddaughter and grandson.

Merryn Howe and I are still great friends and see each other regularly.

Section 39 (1969)
Section Representative:

Liz Jubb (Grant) *As you should all now be aware, I am resigning as Section Rep having been in post for over a decade. If anyone would like to take over, please let me know. Very many thanks to all those who have sent in their news and been so supportive over the years. I have really appreciated it. EJ*

Louise Dixon Our news generally revolves around travelling, which is what we do best! As some people may know, we shuttle backwards and forwards between South Africa and Britain, about four times a year, so in January we decided to make a stopover in Oman. We have a bucket list item which is to visit the major and most unusual opera houses in the world, so when we discovered that there is a beautiful and quite new opera house in Muscat, we simply had to go, especially when we saw that *Madame Butterfly* was being performed the day before Euan's birthday. What a stunning piece of modern, Islamic-style design and what a pleasure to be part of such a blend of music and architecture.

We took the opportunity to have a five-day 4x4 tour in part of Oman, which is very dry, mountainous and beautiful. It reminded us of the huge desert expanses of Namibia. A highlight was getting stuck on the top of a very high soft-sand dune, where we had gone to watch the sunset. Our driver managed to dig our vehicle out, using no more than his bare hands!

The remarkable thing about Oman is that it effectively has a benevolent dictator. The Sultan has been the absolute monarch since 1970 and he has ploughed the country's oil revenues back into developing it, and the people are very loyal and appreciative of what he has done. There are some twelve-hundred castles and forts, which bear testimony to the constant warring in its history.

Some of the grander forts and castles are being restored and are exceptionally beautiful. An unexpected cherry on the cake was that **Jane Clifford's sister, Sally**, arrived in Muscat the day before we flew on to South Africa, so we were able to meet up for a very enjoyable marina-side dinner. If anyone is looking for a winter short break, Oman is certainly worth considering. Direct flights from London with British Airways.

Meanwhile, South Africa continues to wrestle with the aftermath of the Zuma years. Corruption, on a breathtaking scale, has brought the state-owned power generator to its knees and national rolling power cuts have been taking place. It's maddening to see such a beautiful country so badly treated by a group who claimed to be the country's liberators. The General Election is on May 8th and it's hard to know what to hope for!

Sara Freakley (Rubinstein) A huge thank you for all that you have done during your tenure... especially instigating the London get-together a couple of years ago. Like you, life is full on with family (four grandchildren, three of whom live next door), community commitments (chair of the PC, chair of community events committee and Save our Pub team, tennis club organiser etc!), teaching, and finally, artistic endeavours (two exhibitions over the coming year), oh, and I forgot the garden... and of course my husband and LIFE!

Noni Graham (Paton) I am still working but doing quite a lot less than I used to; still a bit of B&B and also some self-catering in our little Garden Studio. I manage our other five rental properties, which isn't very arduous. Otherwise lots of tennis and circuit-training in an effort to keep reasonably fit! Rory, our eldest son, is getting married in London in May to a lovely girl called Flora who he met at Oxford six years ago. Our younger son Neil is now at Homerton College, Cambridge doing a PGCE having spent the last three years teaching English in Madrid. We are so relieved he is finally doing a proper qualification! I am still going beating with my little Cocker spaniels in the shooting season. Can't really think of anything very exciting to tell you!

Caroline Heaton-Watson (McKane) Life continues well for us in Battersea. We now have our daughter's spaniel for the next few years so we're enjoying walks along the Thames, Battersea Park and our small garden. Said daughter and family upped sticks last March from Zug near Zurich for the warmer climes of Kuala Lumpur, hence Hunter coming to stay in London. So now we have two children in the same city but miles away. We are intrepid travellers however and visit a couple of times a year.

Our son has been there six years and by chance a job came up at Epsom College International for our teacher son-in-law. Little granddaughter, nearly three, has started nursery and swims like a fish. We shall go over in April/May and visit Vietnam too: somewhere I've always wanted to see. Our eldest daughter and family live in France with their two children and we help out during the holidays and half-terms. This doesn't leave a lot of time, especially as my husband is still working, but a lot can be done from afar these days. I'm still enjoying my tennis and voluntary work when I'm in London. Celebrated forty years of marriage with a big party in Battersea Park on one of the hottest days of last summer. We invited everyone who came to our wedding all those years ago plus new friends and all the family of course from one year to eighty-nine years old, a wonderful occasion.

A big thank you to Liz for all her work over the years, and keeping us up to the mark, not easy I'm sure!

Heather Jenne In retirement from part-time music instrument teaching, I am carrying on with lots of music making, playing sackbut (an early trombone) in a couple of folk-dance bands and an orchestra and early music group and singing with several choirs and running a church choir. Having also retired from working as a part time maintenance gardener, I am working my allotment more rigorously and revamping my garden (following a visit by Mr Fox to my free-range hens and therefore a decision not to keep them any more). I have also been cooking occasionally for an old folks' community centre and am on my third food hygiene and handling certificate (how have we managed to keep so healthy during all those years of slovenly hygiene?) These activities are currently in abeyance while I care for my husband who has a terminal brain tumour, though the plus side to this is that the children have moved home and are bringing a breath of fresh air and optimism to the situation. *(I know the Section would join me, Heather, in sending you our best wishes and thanks for writing at such a stressful time).*

Liz Jubb (Grant) My news is much the same as always! We continue to enjoy Dorset and are heavily involved in local activities. Last year we visited Phil's grandson who was doing the final year of his law degree at Nijmegen University in Holland. We visited Arnhem (which I regret to say I always thought was in Germany!) and in Nijmegen were taken to the site of a bombing raid in WWII when a school was completely destroyed... only for me to discover this was a 'mistake' by the Allies. It was a salutary history lesson.

We also spent a few days in Amsterdam, but we were glad to escape as it was absolutely heaving and very hot! Said grandson, having got an excellent degree, has now decided he wants to be an airline pilot so is busy training with Easy Jet. So far, he has passed all exams with flying colours (ha ha) so hopefully we will see him in the air before too long.

As most years, we returned to Bude for some lovely R&R in June and in July had a splendid week in Durham where we marvelled at the way the local women dressed up to the nines to go out but were escorted by men who looked as if they hadn't seen a bath in months!!

In September we had a gorgeous two weeks in Portugal, on the Eastern Algarve, with wonderful weather which gave us the opportunity to learn more about a country about which we knew virtually nothing. We rounded off the year with Christmas in Falmouth which was fabulous: glorious apartment, wonderful walks and food and reasonable weather. This year we are off to Washington in May and hopefully Russia later in the year.

On the home front we had a garden makeover last year, so enthusiasm is renewed for being outside and I have purchased loads of new photography gear so have now stepped up a level. Family wise, all are well, my husband still sings with several choirs, the cat continues to rule, and we are getting ready for the visitor season! Finally, I should like to thank all those who have been so good about contributing news each year - I have really appreciated it.

Jo Leadbetter (Salz) A few years away from seventy... definitely time to visit more places on my list. Had a wonderful trip to Paxos with the whole family and recently a delightful visit to Venice. Next stop Istanbul and then Japan. Nothing too extreme yet but a good start. Look forward to our next garden visit with Liz and Clare plus anyone else who might like to join us!

Kate McDowall I have been doing lots of travelling, having just realised that there is possibly only a small window in one's life when there is enough time and money to travel, and the health to do it! Last year was Madeira, Russia, New Zealand and Latvia, this year it is Chicago and Portland Oregon, Puglia, Madrid, and possibly a road trip to Switzerland to see my nephew, who has become something of an expert on crypto currencies and blockchain technology... one has to keep up.

Lyn Moffat (Thomas) Just to say thank you for everything you have done to keep this section together. I don't have a lot of news except to say I am well and happy. One of the horses I have bred is a British Champion which still astonishes me. Life is full of ups and downs, but all the family is currently fine! Two children married and the other in a very long-term relationship. She says they do intend to marry eventually just other stuff keeps getting in the way. Not that marriage is the be all and end all. Surrounded by animals here who are in constant need of attention and looking forward to spring.

Clare Monro (Rust) We are still loving being in Cornwall, although a long way from our offspring in Sussex and Seville. I am enjoying singing with the local choral society (Miss Naylor, eat your heart out) and we are about to sing a wonderful piece by Handel: 'Israel in Egypt'. At a recent book club reading I ended up in the house of **'Liz Rice' née Garvie** who was at Westonbirt seven years or so after me and was daughter of the school Sister, I think. She was an actress, and delightful. Best wishes to **Liz Jubb** for all her hard work on our behalf, thank you Liz.

Carolyn Monty (Tanner) My sons have got me going skiing again after many years' break and it's great. I'm happiest in the mountains. Having spent all of my twenties in and around them, there's no doubt about that. So, I've had to get fitter than normal, and get into my ski pants (refusal to give in I guess). I've been out three times so far this winter 2018/19 and am looking forward to more. I am loving Switzerland again. If life gets difficult, ski!

Daphne Oliver-Bellasis (Parsons) No real news, except that we love our new house. It was quite something to get all the building works done and move out of our house of thirty-eight years, or seventy years in Hugh's case. Feels wonderful now it is done. The local auction house and charity shops have done well. Hopefully we will now have more time to enjoy our three lovely granddaughters (one aged four and twins of two) who live nearby, and get the garden straight.

Jill Powell (Fawkes) Life in Farnham continues to be fun, and I still very much enjoy my tennis; also skiing, walking the dog and gardening. All good activities to keep me reasonably fit and out of mischief! We have recently given a home to a retired working gun dog, aged eight, a black Labrador, Pepper. Although grey around the muzzle, she is still full of beans and has been well trained so is very obedient. John is enjoying his retirement and has recently had his first book published. It is a military history, called *Haig's Tower of Strength* and is about General Edward Bulfin, and his career through the First World War and then afterwards in Palestine. Despite being described by the publishers as for a 'niche market', it is selling quite well, especially in Ireland (Bulfin was, unusually for that time, an Irish Roman Catholic).

If any old girls are in the Farnham area, do get in touch – contact details available through Section Rep or the school.

Kate Roberts I am still managing to live where I have since 2001 and enjoying my little herd of three horses, even though I am not really riding at the moment. Have got some goals for this year, and fingers crossed, I will attain some of them. Last summer just got so hot I gave up!!

Ruth Stark (Worrall) In July 2018 I finished four years as the Global President of the International Federation of Social Workers, an organisation covering one-hundred-and-twenty-eight countries with over three million social workers in membership.

It was a great privilege and I have now turned my hand to writing to share some of the learning I was able to explore in that time. The first anthology will be published by IFSW as an e-book on World Social Work Day, 19 March 2019. I continue to work, mainly with children in the court system and with people facing deportation. I am not sure that I am quite ready to retire yet! My husband, John is not so well; he has been a lifelong smoker. This has restricted travel as he can no longer fly but we do still manage to get away in the campervan. Children and grandchildren are thriving, along with their various animals large and small, and our son, who is into sports and outdoor activities of the adventurous type.

Finally, I want to record thanks to Liz who has worked really hard to keep our section in touch with each other, a job well done!

Liz Speller (Moore), Angie Waite, Carlo Trotter (Sheppard), Denette Matthews (Skeil) and **Tink Carney-Smith (Smallman)** were in touch in February following my initial request for news but are clearly busy people with busy lives so no update from the last time although **Denette** did say she had been travelling in Argentina and the Antarctic (wow!)

Section 38 (1968)

Section Representative:
Chris Shaw (Morris)

Unfortunately, I have to begin with two sad items of news. Firstly, I have learned that **Judith McGill** died in February. I'm afraid I have no further details, but I do know that Judith had been struggling with cancer for several years and had recently had a recurrence. She lived in London. I first met Judith as a ten-year-old in Sedgwick. Our condolences to her family and to her friends.

Secondly, **Alison Gauld (Taylor)** wrote as follows: I am very sorry to have to let you know that my son, Kristian Ward, died in mid-November. So, I am not really up to much at all at present. He was in a very dark place mentally, everything went wrong at once, and he hung himself. It is hard even for me to write this. He did, however, have a lovely obituary in *The Times* on 29th December and *The Telegraph* on 31st November. It was PTSD. He did four trips in Afghanistan.

Many of Alison's old school friends have been in touch with her since hearing this tragic news, and I have also forwarded to her other messages which have been sent to me to pass on. Our love and support go to Ali, to her other son Ashton, and to Kristian's wife and children.

Alison Andrews (Margaret Morgan) also lost her son a few years ago and was quick to get in touch with **Alison (Ali) Gauld**. Alison made the long drive from Scotland (incurring a speeding fine in the process!) to join our fiftieth anniversary reunion in September 2018. It was good to see her after such a long time and I am hoping to meet her again somewhere in the north of England in the autumn.

Penny Bysshe (Osborn) also came to the reunion. She writes: Apart from the great sadness I have felt for my friend Ali I have had a very happy and busy year. I now have two grandchildren as our daughter Julia produced another baby boy in November; we are having a great deal of fun looking after them.

My ballroom and Latin classes are going well, as are the tea dances we run twice a month. We are now spending more time concentrating on improving our Scottish dancing skills. We have joined several Scottish dancing clubs and have a calendar full of Scottish dancing balls, dances and training days. This is all in preparation for an intensive week of Scottish dancing at the summer school we are going to attend at St Andrews in August.

This is a year of festivals: we have just been to our first literary festival in Keswick, which we have thoroughly enjoyed, and we are going to go to the Edinburgh Festival in August, also for the first time. We have sold our house in France, which is good as it frees us up to visit more far-flung holiday destinations before we reach the stage when we may find that the journeys to get there are too daunting to undertake. One highlight of the year was the lovely Westonbirt reunion organised so well by **Chris Shaw**. It was a very happy occasion with lots of laughter and reminiscences.

Deborah Dorrance-King (Dorrance) wrote: I was very saddened to hear of Judith's death. I think I knew that she was ill. I feel very much for Alison

- we never expect our children to die before us, and in such tragic circumstances.

An interesting year. It started off as usual with a trip to Gedarif, Sudan near the Ethiopian border with the usual NGO (Salamat), followed by a week with our son in Falmouth, where we had glorious weather for boat trips and gardens.

In late June my husband was taken seriously ill, thankfully now recovered, and we had a tense week compounded by the fact that our eldest son was stuck in New York. Although his residency and work permit had been approved the paperwork had not come through (the delays under Trump are horrendous) so he could not come home. A lawyer and letters from here finally had his paperwork through just as my husband came home. Under the circumstances he stayed for six weeks, which was lovely.

In August I went to El Obeid in Kordofan on my own as my husband was still not well enough to travel. It was the wet season and I was gently bitten on my leg. Shortly after my return I developed necrotising fasciitis; six weeks, four operations and skin grafts later I came home. I am now almost recovered but last year's trip to San Diego and San Francisco never happened. All three boys, one fiancée and a girlfriend came here for Christmas, the first time in three years we have all been together for a holiday. I was sorry to miss the reunion and hope we can have one in less than ten years' time again. We should not leave it all to Chris - maybe a lunch somewhere relatively central/convenient for most people to get to and home in the same day.

Julia Douglas (Neath) Highlight of the year was the Westonbirt fiftieth anniversary which we celebrated back in September - where has the time gone?! A group of us met up in The Hare and Hounds and after a swift snack we made our way to the school, where we were shown round. The interior of the building is still as grandiose as ever and consequently feels slightly surreal as one gets older! Still, we enjoyed the tour and the promenade around the grounds afterwards. Luckily the weather was lovely, so we saw everything at its best. **Chris Shaw** very kindly put **Judith Kramer (Nettleton)** and myself up in her very comfortable house in Tetbury and we met up with others for a meal at The Close in the evening, so all in all it was a very pleasant outing.

Fortunately, everyone in our family is in good form and we are expecting a fourth grandchild (to be born in Brazil) to join the clan in April. We had a lovely walking and cycling holiday in Austria last June, and then in January/February of this year we spread our wings to Argentina and Chile, where we saw some magnificent scenery in Patagonia.

Jane Fisher (Binney) I continue to do some work both here and in Zimbabwe and Lebanon but am gradually cutting down. We have five grandchildren now, with one family based in Paris, one in Ukraine and two in this country. I still play tennis, table tennis and badminton and have just joined a band!

Di Gale (Forwood) All's well in the Gale household. Both boys employed now and living at home, I hope saving up for the future. I've nearly come to the end of my chairmanship of the local tennis club. Last year was so busy with GDPR raising its ugly head and the LTA bringing out four criteria for affiliation, which involved me rattling off several new policies, mainly on safeguarding-type issues.

I managed to join John on three overseas trips, when I get to do quite a bit of sightseeing on my own. Lots of advantages there, but my best trip was a family one to Venice for my nephew's wedding in September. I'd been there before, but in 1965 when my six photos were black and white, and I was shocked by the colourful beauty of the city this time. St Mark's Square still looks magnificent, having recently been cleaned, and I loved the way the sunlight danced on The Grand Canal. **Annabel Kerr (Johnston)** is coming around tonight; she now has five grandchildren, the oldest is just seven. She is very involved with both families, but we make time for a film night, watching things that the others might not be interested in! **Hilary Hughes (Moore)** managed to handwrite her letter from Brisbane well before Christmas this year - amazing what you can do when you retire! She seems fit and healthy and was seen on television waving her Guernsey flag during the Commonwealth Games. She still enjoys singing with a choir.

I enjoyed last year's AGM, coinciding with the school's ninetieth birthday celebrations. It worked well and was most enjoyable, especially the church service. I was, however, really disappointed with a bad error in the ninetieth anniversary book, especially as it had my name to it! The photo on page forty-two has the wrong names underneath. These should have been with a photo of the Girl Guides Summer 1964, which I'd sent in, hence the mention of our guide leader Miss Mercer. Also, showing that you should never believe everything you read in print, on page fifty-eight it tells about pocket money, BUT, we couldn't draw out the equivalent of 20p because 2 shillings is only 10p, and sixpence is only two and a half pence now. Yes, we survived on 10p per week. As you can see, I have read the book cover to cover. A very enjoyable read. I also bought the book about the Holford family, then read it very carefully so I could send it out to Hilary for her Christmas present! That was most interesting, too. Well worth reading.

Janet Johnson (Plowright) This year I have been collecting choirs and grandchildren, and both are giving me a lot of pleasure. Madrigals, a chamber choir, church choir, etc. In one group I sing alongside **Jane Fisher**'s husband, Simon. Oxford is a very small world. Both our son and our younger daughter live locally - we are very lucky. Freda has two little boys, now just over two and a half years old and five months. The second one was the reason I didn't manage to get to the last reunion. I see them weekly, ostensibly to offer support, but mostly just to enjoy their company. Our elder daughter is expecting her first baby at the end of August. This may mean some trips up north, which I'm looking forward to.

I have seen **Jane** at several concerts; she is a very loyal member of the audience. And I've met up with **Dee** and **Jane** a couple of other times. Apart from that, I'm afraid I haven't been in contact with others from school and am also sorry to have lost contact, for the moment, with **Libba Scott**. I wonder if anyone has any news of her?

My mother turns 100 this year, and we're preparing a family get-together for her. She lives down the road in a very happy residential home, where they patiently accommodate her severe short-term memory loss, and where she is very contented most of the time. My husband continues to enjoy his work as a letter carver in stone, based in a studio in north west Oxfordshire.

Chris Shaw (Morris) Unfortunately, **Ruth** couldn't make the reunion we held last September to mark fifty years since we left Westonbirt. Maybe we are fatter/thinner/greyer than we were, but we still managed to have a great time. The Association AGM had been pulled forward to May to coincide with the school's ninetieth birthday celebrations at fairly short notice, and several of our number couldn't make it, so we decided to stick to our original plan and meet in the autumn. Attendees were **Alison Andrews, Dee Sichel, Jane Fisher, Julia Douglas, Judith Kramer, Penny Bysshe, Iona Gordon** and myself. After meeting at The Hare and Hounds, we proceeded to school where we were greeted by the Head's PA Rhiannon Roche. As it was term-time, we couldn't roam freely, so were given a bespoke tour by a slightly older Old Girl, **Angela Potter (Tracy)** (Section 26), who now lives in Westonbirt, and gives guided tours on a regular basis. I really do recommend these tours, the proceeds go to the Holfords of Westonbirt Trust, which is doing so much to restore the House and gardens. A very worthy cause, and we all agreed that everything looked in better nick than at the time of our fortieth Reunion. It was fascinating to hear things about the House and the Holford family that were either long forgotten or new to us. Angela has written a booklet entitled *Weston Birt House and the Holfords 1665*–2017 which is also highly recommended.

She was very patient with our chatter and reminiscences, which resulted in our tour apparently taking quite a bit longer than the usual one!

One of the highlights for us was a small museum of memorabilia which has been set up in the old Holford bedrooms on the first floor overlooking the gardens. Afterwards we had a cream tea in the library and then walked around the grounds. Later we assembled for drinks at our home in Tetbury and walked up the street to The Close for dinner. Those of us still around met again for coffee the next morning before going our separate ways. Lots of laughter and memories, and renewed bonds, and good intentions to meet more frequently!

Martin and I are starting to spend more time in Tetbury than in Yorkshire. There is always a lot to do; as I write this we have plans to attend a concert in St Mary's Church, Tetbury as part of the Tetbury Music Festival, and next month we shall, for the first time since we have lived here, go to a concert at Westonbirt School - no doubt another memory stirrer! We go occasionally to antiques fairs in Westonbirt House and are frequent visitors to the Arboretum. The latter is a favourite trip for our grandchildren - we now have six as my daughter Suzy had a little girl, Nellie, last July.

One of the happy results of an increased flow of correspondence with everyone in the course of organising the reunion was that I have renewed contact with some of our group who had been 'missing' for a while, and **Iona Gordon** joined us on the day. She lives in Cardiff, and said she was looking forward to organising her daughter's wedding this year. **Jane White (Weston),** who lost her husband at a young age, is happily remarried and living near Kings Lynn. Her daughter and **Dee Sichel's** daughter are married to brothers - small world! Finally, **Heather Hickman (Moffett)** has come back into this Section. She lives near Cirencester, is still nursing and has two small grandchildren - someone else I hope to meet up with this summer.

Diana Sichel (Ferguson) I write from a babysitting week in South London, making bridesmaids' petticoats when Martha is asleep. A rare treat as two-and-a-half is a magic age. I think we are all hanging on for a Brexit answer.

Ruth Watson (Genden) We sold our business, The Crown and Castle in Orford, about eighteen months ago, and it has taken me that long, mentally, to kick the work mode. Or, worse, the guilt at not being constantly on the go. Work can definitely become an addiction as bad as others. Anyway, I am at last enjoying being able to make choices purely predicated on what I want to do, rather than what my work schedule dictates. Having said that, I am currently writing a book about my hotelier/restaurateur life. It's not easy being disciplined without a deadline but I hope to have finished it by the end of the year. I love where I write, in our Billy-lined library next to the duck pond. In winter, with the glazed doors shut, I can watch everything from wild ducks to stoats wend their way to the water's edge, completely oblivious to my presence.

Talking of water, we are in the throes of setting up a business to clear duckweed from ponds, moats and lakes. We see it everywhere in Suffolk, including on our own water, and it is almost impossible to clear, but, hopefully, we have designed a method using a submersible pump. Tests are under way to make sure that it both works and that the necessary equipment is practicable to sell or hire out.

Both David and I are on a 'better gut' diet inspired by Michael Mosley's *Clever Guts* book. It seems to be working as we have lost over a stone apiece since David's seventieth birthday in January and feel a lot springier. Talking of birthdays, neither of us can believe that we met aged twenty-six and twenty-seven. Thank God one has no concept of age and the ageing process when young! The only good thing about it is that you're not actually dead.

On that cheery note, we had the entire house painted over a five-week period in January and February. It was painful but forced us to clear out some no-go areas. So now we can delight in renewed and refreshed living quarters minus a lot of crud. Mind you, we sent quite a lot of things that had been stored for decades to auction. (Cheffins in Cambridge were excellent - no connection!) The house and garden are far too big but sod it, we adore living here and will only move when we can't afford gardening help. I've already identified the space for a tiny lift should it become necessary. (Installing a stair lift would be over my dead body, literally - they're so damned ugly).

I have been in intermittent contact with **Lindsay Costello (Bryan)** and this year we have decided we really must get together. I think we're both frightened of how we'll look, not having seen each other for some forty-five years.

Section 37 (1967)
Section Representative:
Jenifer Davidson (Moir)

Sultan Al-Quaiti (Rashid) Sooty is greatly looking forward to our year's reunion in Studland this Autumn. Her UK charity Friends of Hadhramaut goes from strength to strength by the grace of God and she hopes to see at least some of you at Cressing Temple Barns in Essex on 14th September:

www.hadhramaut.co.uk.

Her daughter **Fatima** (ex-Westonbirt) and **Maija Calvert** (also ex-Westonbirt) are trustees of the charity. The charity's fundraising dinner in Bonn last September attracted sixty-five guests.

Alison Boxley (Muir) A group of us enjoyed a fun reunion last May. We have one every year for our year group and have been to many interesting and varied places. 2018 was kindly hosted by Jenifer in her spacious Edinburgh house. Lovely weekend including a walk up to Arthur's Seat.

This year, most of us are turning seventy and choosing to celebrate this milestone in different ways. I decided that it was impossible to have one celebration as I am based in New Zealand, my daughters and granddaughter are in Australia, brother in Greece and sister and many good friends are in England. So, I'm having seventy celebrations of various sorts and sizes. I started on my sixty-ninth birthday and will carry on till the end of 2019. Twenty-five done so far!

Our annual Westonbirt reunion will be a bit grander than previous ones to mark the great age that we've achieved. Three days in Dorset in October courtesy of **Sarah Ferguson**. Report in next year's news.

Jenifer Davidson (Moir) I seem to be as busy as ever – still working part-time and doing various voluntary jobs. Sadly, one of the playgroups for which I am Finance Administrator had to close at the end of last year due to lack of pupils. The government's new hours for pre-school children is causing havoc in that sector. I am also still playing a lot of tennis and doing aqua-fit.

Our reunion in Edinburgh in May was great fun and we had wonderful weather. There's a photo somewhere to prove that most of us (not me) made it to the top of Arthur's seat! It was lovely to have everyone here - **Alison Boxley (Fowler), Cas Boddham-Whettam (Burkitt), Hilary Davis (Stone), Christine MacLaren, Vanessa Pugh, Ruth Precious (Richards), Jane Hill (Rust), and Budgie Savage.** Sadly, **Daphne Sanders** was unable to join us at the last moment.

Hilary Davis (Stone) For once I have got some news for you! Andrew and I became grandparents for the first time in February this year, when Lewis James Davis was born. Our elder son Matthew and his wife Sarah are absolutely delighted, as are we. I may have mentioned that I was working towards an MA in History with the Open University: I submitted my dissertation on the Mormon mission in Herefordshire that took place during 1840 and I am very pleased to say that I have just been awarded the MA. It is a fascinating topic, but I am really glad to have completed it!

It was lovely to see everyone for our reunion in Edinburgh last year and I also went to lunch at **Eileen's** house with **Sue Ross, Judy Chesterman, Karen Olsen and Alison Parry**, who had not been able to come up to Edinburgh. I very much enjoy catching up with everyone and I am looking forward to the Dorset reunion in October.

Christine MacLaren I am in Cyprus at the moment, on a 'cultural' tour of the north. Plenty of ruins, just not very warm! We had several interesting trips last year, to Egypt, Japan and Cape Verde and later this year we are going to Peru.

We took American relatives to Scotland last September with highlights being several days on Iona, visiting the MacLaren territory around Balquhidder and seeing a MacLaren headstone at Culloden. We are repeating the exercise, minus Iona, with another American relative in April!

We are also hoping that Jamie will get his PhD at the end of April; what he will do with it is anyone's guess!

Hilary Davis (Stone) and I have met up a few times in the last year. I hope she will tell you about her studies and about becoming a grandparent!

Looking forward to the October reunion.

Sue Pasfield (Ross) Still in denial about getting older, and still enjoying life. I hope this is not associated with still being a working woman, because someday I would like to stop! We have a software company with employees (always think twice about hiring staff!) selling training to law firms in the USA.

I got Lyme disease three years ago but am now largely better. I say this in case anyone else, or their family, has fallen prey to tick bites and Lyme and would like to discuss it. Contact me if you'd like to talk. *(You can contact her through her Section Rep or the school).*

Section 36 (1966)
Section Representative:
Julia Braggins (Cock)

It has been lovely to hear from so many of you again: thank you for making my job so easy and interesting.

Moi Beveridge (Adamson) Probably worst or second worst year of my existence so shall not dwell on it. Anyway, almost finished. On my way back to London and having very small flat done up for me. Nearly all my life has been full of parasites so have decided to be my one and only parasite for what remains of my sojourn on earth. Got rid of so many artefacts and general possessions as really didn't/don't need them. Luckily retained membership of the Hurlingham Club so can go and moulder there! Anyway, a new life beckons so here I go! I will try and make the effort to make reunion next year. New London address from mid-March *(please contact Section Rep or the school for new contact details)*. Had it for years and luckily didn't sell as no way I could buy now - twelve minutes' walk to Sloane Square and right behind a large Waitrose!

Julia Braggins (Cock) A happy year of celebrations, for me – seventieth birthday (in common with lots of our year) and our golden wedding, which, as I think I said last year, made me feel antique. We celebrated with a wonderful trip to Canada (first time), to the Rockies, and then to spend time with my sister's stepson just outside Toronto. The whole thing was marvellous. All well with our younger family members, grandchildren aged four to eleven now, and we all had a great week in Norfolk together last summer, to be repeated this year. They won't want to come away with the oldies for ever, so we're making the most of it now. Heading for my second knee replacement in a month's time. No doubt I'll be gambolling like a spring lamb next time I write. Still working for Samaritans, as a trustee for local Citizens' Advice, and also taking the minutes for the All-Party Parliamentary Group on penal affairs. Always interesting, though having to fight my way through the Brexit demonstrators just now. How will it all pan out? Have had glimpses of **Sandy Marshall (Hellawell)**, **Judy Turner (Marryat)**, see below, and also **Jo Clarke (Brooke)** this year. Always great to catch up.

Judy Chesterman (Clarke) Well here we are – three score years and ten! I'm enjoying the amazing new lease of life my hip replacement two years ago has given me and Arthur is striding around happily on his two new knees. Just as well, as the latest grandchild was born in June 2018, a little boy this time, William Alexander. Mark and Katrina have upped sticks and left London for a bigger house in Somerset to cope with their expanding family. The eldest, Sophia, is now six and Isabel is less than two years older than her brother, so it's quite a handful. We still seem to see a great deal of them, but in more concentrated doses. Emma keeps pretty well, although her ME comes back to bite her if she gets a cold. Her Spanish academic translation work is flourishing, and her massage business is also doing well, so it's good to see her getting along okay.

Sarah Ferguson In March last year I joined some fellow freestyle skiing competitors ('78 World Cup vintage) for ski touring from a yacht sailing around north west Iceland. This was my second week's skiing in twelve years; confirmation that my knees had repaired after a ten-year rest and that skiing with old friends in NZ in August was realistic. This was so successful I will be going again this August, a great time to be away from the tourist season at home and celebrate freedom from the hotel business. The garden at Studland Bay House and soft fruit and veggies at my home still give pleasure and the produce still enjoyed. In November I spent time in Goa at Purple Valley Ashtanga Centre with Joey Miles, my favourite yoga teacher, before returning to Wanaka, NZ for their summer. I'm writing this as I introduce my nineteen-year-old niece Lucy to her Kiwi cousins, mountain bike the excellent trails, and prepare to return home for springtime. I look forward to welcoming our year to Studland Bay House for a reunion in October.

Lucy Fisher (Sadleir) Life is treating me well on the whole. A year ago, my latest granddaughter was born in Sweden, Aida, to join four-year-old Laurie. Their parents, son Tim, and Jenny, decided to spend six months of her maternity leave travelling round Europe with the family in a twenty-six-year-old camper van! I joined them in Sicily in October to celebrate Tim's fortieth and had a wonderful time. As I write I'm flying to Copenhagen to stay several days with them in Malmö, Sweden. Daughter, Zoe, lives with her husband, Bob, and six-year-old Bethan in Worcester. I collect Bethan from school once a week which is great, and see the family then. My boyfriend, Ian, celebrated his seventieth last year and he and I had a lovely sunny week in South Wales last June and two fabulous weeks in the south Dordogne in September. This was preceded by my godson's wonderful wedding on the Isle of Wight and a Ruby Wedding in Cornwall in August which enabled us to visit **Jeni Whittaker** for lunch.

Alexandra Marshall (Hellawell) Like many of our vintage, activities seem to be similar from year to year – though one is grateful for still being able to bend and balance a bit and keep one's place in an auditioned choir. Gloucester Choral Society was privileged to take part in the Philharmonia's celebratory concert for Parry's centenary at the Festival Hall last May. 'Jerusalem' was magnificent, as I remember it always was at the end of term when we would flatten ourselves against the sides of the hall. Why was it essential to squash ourselves so far back? Another memory surfaced as I read **Eleanor Fountain's (Bateman)** entry. I came to Westonbirt in the summer term, when friendship groups had already been formed. I found it hard to keep up mentally and physically – all that learning of vespers and fire whistles, making conversation at table and rushing from one end of the building to the other, without running. Very early in that term there was a treasure hunt, and I found myself being shepherded kindly by **Eleanor** and **Sian Davies**, senior to me, upper fourths, and athletic. I was a huge encumbrance to them, fell over and generally couldn't keep up. They were patience personified, and in spite of it all, we won the event.

Back in the recent past, **Jules (Braggins), Judy Turner (Marryat)** and I met at The Vyne in June last year. Only the ground floor was open at the time, which was maybe just as well as we took half an hour to get past the interesting old map in the hall and would still be there now had it all been open!

We had a holiday with the family in Arran, the first time we'd done this. It was great, and the children were instructed not to come bouncing in at dawn.

We explored the Republic of Ireland, also a first. I had had in mind an elegant chamber concert in the candlelit splendour of an Ascendancy house, but instead we ended up in a village at the end of the road on the Atlantic coast in time for Storm Hector. A wonderful place – maybe this year we'll make the chamber concert.

Karen Olsen My great-niece, Sasha Elizabeth, arrived safely by Caesarean section in February 2018. Her mother, my niece, had been suffering from placenta praevia during her pregnancy which meant that a Caesarean birth was the only option. It was a worrying time for us all, especially my sister **Jackie Woodgate (Olsen)** who spent a couple of months in London helping out.

Anyway, we are a year on and have just celebrated her first birthday and although she is still petite, Sasha is a laid-back and happy little baby who spends a lot of time smiling and having a little chuckle to herself. They all moved back to the west country in the summer and are now in North Somerset, not far from us all.

I had a weekend with **Judy Chesterman (Clarke)** in London early in June 2018 and we had lunch on the Saturday at the home of **Eileen McGregor (Bond),** joined by **Sue Pasfield (Ross), Alison Parry (Sturdy-Morton)** and **Hilary Davis (Stone).** A great chance for a catch-up.

Alison Parry (Sturdy-Morton) Continued with my travels starting in February with an amazing road trip through New Zealand. What an incredible country: fabulous scenery, interesting history, exquisite wines, heavenly food, totally delightful people and so much more. A big thank you to everyone for your suggestions of places to visit... am so glad I got to Stewart Island and saw emus on the beach at midnight.

Enjoyed catching up with **Sarah Ferguson** in Wanaka and look forward to our class reunion with her in Dorset in 2019.

I am definitely catching up on my bucket list. In October I went on an expedition to Antarctica and finally got to visit The Falklands, which has family history. Antarctica was beyond extraordinary... not just being so close to nature, outrunning a hurricane (got the certificate) and swimming in the icy waters of Deception Island (another certificate) but also the uninhabited vastness and with no other boat in the vicinity (we were the first ship of the new season), the power of nature and the fickleness of the weather. The beauty of nature whether it is whales, penguins, seals or southern specific birds. The colours of the ice and sea. The dryness of the cold. The inquisitiveness of the different penguins, most of whom were inspecting humans for the first time and were totally unafraid and probably pretty unimpressed by our identical knee-high rubber boots. Seeing Elephant Island where Shackleton's men had survived, sailing along beside A-68 the world's largest iceberg (5,800 square kilometres of solid moving ice), changing course as the sea turned to ice around us as a hurricane was fast approaching. Then battening down the hatches to cross the Bering straits to Cape Horn, Drake's passage, Tierra del Fuego and Ushuaia. A geography and history lesson all wrapped up in stormy seas. I loved every minute of the expedition.

Another road trip in December in the USA with my daughter and grandchildren, exploring some of California and Arizona. Wild deserts and cowboy country - a great success for all. And, yes, we saw the infamous 'wall'. We then flew to Washington DC for Christmas with my daughter-in-law's family. On Christmas Day the young were doing their gym moves and somersaults and I forgot my age and fractured my sternum in the process. Very painful, slow and invisible recovery. Very thankful for ibuprofen, as I have had to just keep on going, changing a few habits and continuing to enjoy life.

Am still having fun with my silversmithing and exploring the theatrical scene in London.

Tilly Roberts I celebrated my seventieth last year by inviting my two children and their families to Rapa Nui, formerly known as Easter Island. We were seven in all so spent a few nights at my place in Santiago before flying out over the Pacific at the crack of dawn. July was the perfect time to go as we had fabulous weather and access to everything without too many crowds. We visited all the Moai, craters, museums, caves and Anakena Beach, having rented two jeeps. With super guide book in hand, one of the grandchildren would read to us all about the place we were in.

It was a really fun holiday for all ages and no-one used their mobile phones! Two went diving whilst the rest admired the turtles and puffer fish from the dock. I highly recommend this to anyone wanting a family holiday.

Diane Stibbard (Brocklehurst) We continue to visit New Zealand over the New Year to stay in our idyllic home on the lakeside shrouded by Coronet Peak, and with the town of Queenstown in walking distance away. It is lovely to get summer sunshine and long days. I have had another spell of breast cancer and am in remission, as well as an ongoing back problem, with neuralgia affecting both legs. What it is with advancing years. I will be seventy this year. Harriet is finishing London Business School in July and has been given a place at Citibank and was given a scholarship. Helena has very excitably moved into a very new home with a delightful husband. They are off to the Andaman Islands, for a second time, on holiday today.

Section 35 (1965)
Section Representative:
Marilyn Jones (Bird)

News from **Marilyn Jones (Bird)**

Only one person sent me their news this year; hopefully more next year!

Sian King (nee Davies) writes 'Although engaged in a wide range of voluntary activities, none of them are quite like paid employment which I very much miss following retirement five years ago. The most fulfilling recreational activity is doing a part-time PhD, examining the production and distribution of chapbooks in seventeenth century South Wales, which is where I now live. This involves visiting a range of libraries and archives, as well as a great deal of internet research, and, of course, writing it all up. I also enjoy mentoring young librarians who are compiling portfolios in order to apply to become Chartered Members of CILIP (Chartered institute of Libraries and Information Professionals) and, for the same organisation, chairing a group meeting the needs of retired members throughout the UK.'

As for **myself**, eight grandchildren keep us on our toes with fun, laughter and babysitting!
    Have had two lovely cruises in the Caribbean in the past four months which provided great contrast.

Section 34 (1964)

Section Representative:
Julia Popham (Bishop)

Ann Beattie (Buckland) We have enjoyed doing trips to Aldeburgh, Harrogate and Charmouth in the last year.

As Canterbury is on the high-speed line to St Pancras, we can be in London in less than an hour. This means we can easily visit the British Museum and the British Library, where we are members, and exhibitions are therefore free.

Mary Cave (Rawlence) Elisabeth Ells writes on Mary's behalf to say, 'My sister Mary Cave (Rawlence) has just become a grandmother for the first time – twins, no less'. Many congratulations to Mary.

June Cohen (nee Kefford) A year of very highs and very lows for me. The highs being: the birth of another beautiful grandchild, our seventh, and third son for our daughter and son-in-law; eldest granddaughter took up her place to read Maths at Jesus College, Oxford, where she is loving every minute, which is filled with a healthy mix of rugby, rowing, great social life and, oh yes,…some Maths; a very happy reunion for our year at Helen Faircliffe's, in September; and a new hip for me in August!
The real low has been the very rapid decline in health for my husband, Clive, who is now seriously ill with a chronic and hugely debilitating disease. Life, as we knew it a year ago, is now unrecognisable. Our four wonderful children have been, and are being, just amazing with their help and loving support. We are very blessed.

Charlotte Essex (Humpidge) In great haste as Richard and I are just off to Thailand with Jonathan and Gail to meet her Thai parents. It will be quite an experience as neither of us have visited the country before. They were married at Blaise Castle Museum in October - a happy occasion with a reception afterwards including a mixture of Thai and English food.

Andrew celebrated his fiftieth birthday, holding a barbecue in Jonathan's garden with others, including many of his old Scouting friends, which was another happy and relaxing day. Catherine joined us for a holiday in Corfu visiting Corfu Town on National Union Day with a ceremony of local dignitaries, parades of brass bands and people in traditional colourful costumes.

We continue with antique fairs, but not quite as many as in previous years, and of course the garden keeps us active!

Susan Fisher (Barritt) Not much to report - still enjoying retirement by the sea and also spending time at our flat in London, the best of both worlds! We keep ourselves active and busy and are very grateful that we have the health to do that.

Ann Grocock This has been a relatively quiet year for me having come to the end of my NHS role at the end of January 2018. I am still chairing a Nuffield charity and that has kept me pretty busy. I was pleased to come to the Westonbirt ninetieth birthday event last May but was very sorry not to be able to get to the London party that **Helen Faircliff** held at her house. During the year I have met up several times with **Chris Bryan** when she has been over from the US. Bill and I have not travelled very much this year as he is getting less mobile, but we have enjoyed holidays in Dorset and spending time with his children and grandchildren.

Claire Marshall If you are a choral aficionada then mark July 2023 in your calendar. The Latvian National Choral Festival happens every five years in Riga. I attended last summer and believe it will prove to be the most glorious choral event of my life: concerts every night; in halls, arenas, and parks; massive craft markets; dancing in the streets; culminating in 14,000 singers on their massive outdoor stages, performing for four hours for some 40,000 people, followed by a grand sing-along from midnight to dawn! The outpouring of human sound contrasted deeply with a visit to Haida Gwaii, remote islands off Canada's West Coast, where abandoned villages of the indigenous peoples crumble softly back to nature. The history was not pretty though the scenery magnificent. On the home front, I entered my last year as Chair of OrKidstra, a volunteer position which keeps me thoroughly occupied. We now have 700 inner-city kids on the programme and have well-developed plans to double over the coming years.

Again, all our graduates went on to post-secondary education in disciplines such as medicine, business, law and even music! All WBs understand the benefit of music in academic and social development. I just wish more educators here had the same conviction. Music is almost absent in the schools until very late on, and then only as an option.

I was happy to see **Liz Davies** when passing through the UK on my return from Latvia. **Helen** kindly offered her home although she was away. Living there was strange as her presence permeates the very walls. Wish the timing had coincided with the reunion, but I was certainly there in 'spirits', (yes, plural!)

Julia Popham (Bishop) Thank you very much to everyone in our Section who replied with their news this year. It is greatly appreciated. Nigel and I had a wonderful holiday last year when we were fortunate enough to do a riverboat cruise between St Petersburg and Moscow and we found it absolutely fascinating.

Our son and daughter-in-law and family are planning to move to Hampshire in the summer and our daughter Clare is now qualified as a children's social worker and is working in Newham, where she finds the work very challenging but rewarding. I have been in touch with **Joyce Seaman (Carnegie) Lella Fountaine (Bateman) and Vicki Schaerer (Lang).**

Christine Schoeb (Bryant) I have moved to my final (?) resting place here in Florida - or at least a new modern home downtown where I can walk to most places, quite a luxury in this country. Still, when unreality strikes, getting back to the gritty grind of daily life in London brings me back to my senses.

Joyce Seaman (Carnegie) We have been contemplating moving back into Oxford from Asthall, near Burford, for several years and have finally done it. We bought a 1970s house which we have taken down and are building a new one, which should enable us to remain living in it, even if we cannot get upstairs in the future. It should be finished by Christmas, and in the meantime, we are renting in Iffley and are delighted with a short bus ride, instead of a commute of up to an hour, to get to work.

Section 33 (1963)
Section Representative:
Helen Faircliff (Wienholt)

Sandra Russell (Morris) was "just packing to go off to New Zealand to see our youngest son and family and really looking forward to it. All well here; still playing quite a bit of bridge at three different clubs; attending Arts Society lectures and special days; and generally keeping pretty busy in the garden and house, and entertaining friends. Always good to keep up with other WB's'."

Mary Gillam (Woodrow) We celebrated our golden wedding anniversary this summer with a lunch party in our garden and a few days at a wonderful family hotel in Dorset in October half term with all the family. We spend a lot of time in Cornwall with the grandchildren. Most of our time is spent looking after our four acres and our two rehomed German shorthair pointers but it keeps us fit.

Helen Faircliff (Wienholt) The form reunion took place in September and I think it shows the strengths of long friendships (since 1957 for some of us) that sixteen of us came together for lunch. In no particular order they were **Bridget Wilson, Liz Edwards, Jane Witt, Helen Wienholt, Di Hughes, Caroline Beloe, Prue Taylor, Susie Iliffe, Mandy Smith, Liz Constance, June Kefford, Anita Armstrong, Suz Bradbury, Julia Tingle, Sue Hyman, Alannah Hall.**

My year has been relatively quiet. I used my caravan a lot and spent a month in Spain (the highlight being hijacked twice in one day - beware the Autopista-7!) and six weeks in France which was really good, and I continued with my French lessons and did a patisserie course. Éclairs, anyone?

However, my peace and quiet is likely to be shattered very soon as I am about to become a granny in April.

Jane Simpson (Witt) 2018 brought forth our sixth grandchild, a second daughter, called Ophelia, for our son Angus, which was very exciting. We now have two grandsons and four granddaughters, so lots to keep us on our toes.

Sadly, we lost our golden retriever in the late summer aged fifteen and a half and the house seems very empty without her. It is the first time in our married life we have been without a dog, but we hope to find another soon, maybe a rescue dog if we can find one that is good with small children.

The reunion held at **Helen**'s house was great fun though sadly **Liz Graley** and I arrived rather late from the west country so didn't have as long to chat to everyone as we would have wished. We subsequently went on holiday to Majorca and met up with **Anita Armstrong** and spent an enjoyable evening with her.

No great holiday plans at the moment as John is awaiting a new hip and walking any distance at all is just too difficult, so looking forward to a good summer in the garden.

Casha McNab (Robertson) I suppose we are all getting that bit older! Just sending you a quick update though the news is all pretty boring! I was down at the Arboretum in September so called in and had a walk round the grounds. Strange to be back. Feel I should spend a little more time and go inside and see what they have done.

Am writing this in the BA lounge on my way back from Australia. Feeling the cold! Had two weeks in Melbourne as our daughter works for Tennis Australia as a physio and is stationed there for the tournament. Our news basically is that we have had two new grandchildren, one of which is in Aus. And we are just embarking on building a new house on our tennis court. So, this year will be busy doing that. Just hope we manage to sell our current home. Brexit is making things very uncertain. Still playing tennis competitively but it gets harder every year! Still I feel it is good for me to get fit. And I play three hours on Tuesday nights.

Julia Tingle 2018 was an uneventful year, except for wondering what awaited us all on April Fool's Day 2019.

My own life was, thankfully, uneventful and happy, so I can recommend rescue dogs such as Pebbles, my Parsons Terrier, as a counterbalance against politicians and political games – particularly because they make you smile every time you enjoy their antics!

I continue being a parish councillor but am not sure for how much longer - the feeble planning laws, and the deep pockets of developers are so depressing that I would rather not know that they are flouting the system without let or hindrance. Every week there is an example of how badly we need the CPRE (Campaign for the Protection of Rural England). I belong to the Sussex branch who are vigilant about fracking, building on brownfields instead of greenfields, or greenbelt (yes!) or over-development (10,000 houses planned nearby). I wonder how many are affordable.

I continue teaching English at the hotel where I used to work. The EU staff are mainly Polish or Romanian. A million Poles still live in the UK, although some are returning because of the improved Polish economy and also fears about their treatment after Brexit because of the disastrous mishandling of public relations by this government, which has given them a sense of alienation and insecurity. As we all know, without the EU staff we could not run hospitals or hospitality. The next largest population who have settled in the UK are Romanians, driven here by corruption and lack of opportunities in their own country. I suspect the same is true of Bulgarians, as their Government sells passports to anyone wishing to enter the EU, as does the Maltese Government.

On a positive note, the year's highlight was a very successful and happy reunion day hosted by **Helen Faircliff** in her home in September. Loyal support was provided by her son and his wife. Most of us found it difficult to recognise those we had not seen for years, but some were, thankfully, instantly recognisable! The food was outstanding – someone must have been attending Domestic Science lessons all those years ago!

Suz Burroughs (Bradbury) I have bad news in as far as my daughter has breast cancer. It was discovered in November when she had the lumps and all the nodes on one side removed. She has just had her second dose of chemo and her treatment will go on until September. Hope the problem will be sorted by then.

I went on a cruise down to the Canaries. Had Force 10/11 going down through the Bay of Biscay and a swell of 6/7 metres off Portugal on the way back up. The weather was not a problem for me and I enjoyed the company and food! It's hard work thinking of shopping and cooking again!

Liz Davies (Edwards) It was wonderful to see so many old friends at **Helen**'s in September. We were blessed with a beautiful day and it was a perfect setting for much chatter, laughter, and catching up. Everyone looked so well it was hard to believe how many decades had passed since we first met, many at Sedgwick.

I remain in Weybridge where Mike and I continue in good health. Both children live reasonably close and we are able to see our two grandchildren frequently.

Ros Barham (Jakeman) This last year we've lurched from one crisis to another. It started with the boiler breaking down to coincide with the arrival of the 'beast from the east' last February when we were without heating or hot water for four weeks! Grim.

However, when not facing problems, I've enjoyed spending time with our four granddaughters, (11, 6, 4 and eighteen months), singing with Guildford Choral, walking miles with my eighteen-month-old Cavalier King Charles, and pottering in the garden. The highlight for 2019 is an invitation to attend a garden party at Buckingham Palace in May! Very exciting.

Anita Dudley (Armstrong) I really enjoyed our reunion in September and continued it into Mallorca by having dinner with **Jane 'Witt'** and her husband.

We've had great weather so far, this year. Just had an excursion to a snail farm. They apparently reproduce by necking and changing sex!

Anthea Shipley (Franklin-Adams) I am enjoying having the children and grandchildren living within five miles of us. Doing carriage driving for the disabled and my daughter likes to compete on my Irish cob with me as the back stepper… great fun!

Sue Coveney (Hyman) I've had the most amazing adventure travelling around Colombia to visit friends in Bogotá, Medellín and Cartagena. All three have a different climate.

After the initial day, being in such high altitude, (Bogotá is the third highest capital in the world) I understood the charm and history of the city. The Colombians are so friendly and welcoming. I don't remember learning anything with Miss Venning about South America! The Botanical Gardens are very beautiful in both Bogotá and Medellín.

We went down a disused salt mine in the mountains in Nemocón near Bogotá. There is now a cave in the mine which contains a chapel for weddings.

In Medellín we took two cable cars up a mountain to fifty-four acres of woodland. The sloths are very shy and mostly come out at dusk. Orchids grew on the bark of very tall trees.

Cartagena is so stunning and is on the Caribbean. Many cocktail bars so I enjoyed gin and tonics and mojitos costing about £1.50 Happy Hour... Some people in Colombia had heard about Westonbirt Arboretum.

Section 32 (1962)

Section Representative:
Sarah Rundle (Milner)

Denise Bittolo (Porter) Life continues much the same in sunny Italy... We are now apparently in recession but it would appear that most of the rest of Europe are heading that way too. It makes us all wonder if the European Union was really a wise choice or not. We have not been fortunate with our governments over the last few years and the present one is really leading us astray. Unfortunately, the Italian population as a whole is very docile, with an attitude of live and let live and no-one rebels.

We had another very hot summer last year and we eventually went over to visit our eldest son and family in Tenerife. Spent the month of November there, the weather being perfect. Nice and sunny but not too hot. Our eldest grandson is there and will be ten in March. It is wonderful seeing him speaking fluent Spanish as well as Italian and also English and German. Although we miss the family lots, they have so many more opportunities than they would have had in Italy.

Our fourth grandchild was born on January 9th Finally, a girl after three boys - Martina! She is only a month old but is already being spoilt by her father and two older brothers.

If anyone is ever passing through Naples, we would love to see you.

Elizabeth Bryant More visits to the Isles of Scilly and Sicily in 2018, the latter to Ortigia, near Syracuse. I spent a couple of weeks in Georgia and Armenia about which I knew nothing. I had an interesting chat with a Londoner whose family had fled Armenia before the genocide and were subsequently forced out of Egypt and Sudan before settling in Britain. It was his first visit to his family homeland.

I went to Berlin again, visiting friends and getting to Potsdam, before a few days in Bamberg seeing more friends. And finally, a few days staying with Aussie friends near Brussels.

My cats and the garden seem to have been rather neglected in the last year. The most exciting days of the year were in Venice at the time of the fourth highest flood for one hundred and fifty years. I spent more than three hours trying to get to my hotel, close to San Marco, which was thigh-high in water. In the end I gave up, got back to the station and took a water taxi to the hotel where we were celebrating a sixtieth birthday. Their lobby was about eighteen inches deep in water, but they managed an excellent dinner and found me a room for the night. During my travels, at Arsenale, I met an American with her eighty-six-year-old mother who couldn't get to their Airbnb. She said they would just wait till the tide went down a bit and then send out a dove.

I continue to enjoy excellent concerts at the Wiltshire Music Centre, theatre and cinema in Bath, and walks round Stourhead. **Mary Hudson** and I still meet regularly, and we had lunch with two Holford contemporaries, each of us talking loudly over the others and laughing a lot as we tried to remember who was who at school. We all agreed not to mention Brexit or Trump. I'm going to Paris for a few days in March and to Copenhagen early in April. I hope to see **Phil Shaw (Northcroft)** in-between times.

Mary Hudson Nothing new to report again. The garden still grows apace and it's getting harder to keep up with it as ever! But choir is going well with two more concerts planned (locally only!) for this year. Otherwise continuing to meet up with a few old Westonbirt friends as and when.

Jyotipakshini - aka Erica Rigg (Harding) I don't have much news this year. My main delight is in my new left hip which is wonderful; it doesn't feel any different from my original (right) one and is just as flexible. I can now climb hills, go to the gym and sleep comfortably. Hurrah for modern medicine and the NHS.

Michael and I are well (touch wood) although a number of our friends and cousins have sadly died in the last few years, which makes us very aware of making the most of now. We are off to Madeira on Monday with this thought in mind!

Sarah Rundle (Milner) A sad year. Robin, my wonderful husband and best friend for fifty-four years died in March. He had been ill for a while and we were coping but then unfortunately NHS administration removed his wonderful carers, brought in less experienced ones, and as a result of this he developed sepsis and died. We were advised to make a complaint and our case was taken up by an extremely helpful and supportive lady from the NHS. As a result of her 'delving' we have received an apology and a promise that 'procedures and protocols' will be changed. I can't ask for more than that. I am lucky to have a very supportive family, I couldn't have managed without them; they, together with my two golden retrievers, keep me going. I am still singing in a local choir and working at Caerhays Castle Gardens. As well as working there when the gardens are open in the spring, I am now helping with work on the archives, which is fascinating.

How I agree with **Sue Whitfield** about Brexit. Daughter and family who live and work in France are devastated at what is happening and have applied for French citizenship. Granddaughter was hoping to study to be a vet in the UK, but time will only tell if that will be possible.

Eldest daughter, Claire, grandson, and I visited Westonbirt Arboretum in the autumn and Claire insisted on driving down the drive, marched in and asked if we could look round! We were welcomed and shown around, and so many memories came flooding back. The Library, Reading Room and Dining Room hadn't changed at all!

Susan Whitfield (Bottomley) It has been another busy year, in our case dominated by both Brexit and a dear little new grandchild not far away called Persephone, or Persie for short. This brings the ratio up a bit, with four girls to seven boys. With one more of my children yet to start a family I do not know when it will all end, but time will tell, and my role is to cuddle and coo and be amazed at the endless flow of love which bursts out and grows round each new baby. The Brexit issue is utterly different – total agony, and since Robert is deeply involved with the Gloucestershire groups working for a People's Vote (together with his work elsewhere to encourage the formation of an elected World Parliament to tackle the things countries cannot do alone) he is kept pretty busy. I support from the sidelines, and on London marches and hold my head in my hands in despair, along with so many others.

I stopped being a governor at Westonbirt last year, staying on a bit longer than planned while the arrangements went through for the move to be part of the Wishford Schools group. I am sure this is the right thing for the school's future and will be interested to see the move to co-education from September, starting with the eleven-year-olds. Two young neighbours recently joined Westonbirt Prep and love it there. My involvement with the Teaching Staff Trust continues; and nearer home, with the retirement of our vicar, I have been involved as churchwarden with the process of appointment of a new one. The advertisement is about to be published as I write (February) and the benefice of three parishes waits with bated breath for applicants to our lovely Cotswold benefice, but meanwhile all are getting on merrily during what is known technically as the vacancy.

We are fortunate in being in good health, and I hope to improve mine further by wallowing in alpine thermal baths at a ski resort in April. We are going for other family members to ski, but I have lazier plans, as well as spending some relaxing time with the three grandchildren involved if they ever stop skiing. I am travelling by train alone for a slightly shorter period within the week and am looking forward to the stress-free reading opportunities.

Last year, **Deb Soper** was over from Guernsey, and we went to the AGM and Picnic in the Park on a lovely, though windy, day. It was tremendous fun, but unfortunately, I cannot go again this year as it clashes with time away. It was a pleasure to see **Gay (nee Durston)** after more than half a century and her husband, and we greatly enjoyed the garden.

Gay Woodley (Durston) A much better year with only one operation, this time on my eye! Successful, but my eyesight is not brilliant.

We had three nephews getting married abroad last summer so we made a holiday around each location, in Croatia, the South of France and Valladollid in Spain

Helen Bianchi joined me again on the autumn opera class trip to Berlin. Three operas in three opera houses, art and history. My first visit to the Jewish museum, which was outstanding and so well designed and for a complete contrast, picturesque Sanssouci Palace and Potsdam.

I really enjoyed the celebrations at Westonbirt in May, meeting up with **Sue Whitfield** and **Deb Soper** whom I hadn't seen for ages. The music performed by the children was of a very high standard. It will be interesting to see how the school develops when it becomes a mixed senior school. The next day we spent a wonderful morning in the Arboretum sampling the elevated walkway for the first time and enjoying the azaleas and rhododendrons; we will be going again in the autumn with our gardening group.

I continue with Rutland Arts Society, the PCC and fund raising for the local hospice as well as a stint on the committee of the garden group. Nevill Holt Opera opened its new theatre last June, which is truly magnificent in a most stunning location. Very good opera performances by young singers, well worth a visit to the East Midlands.

Section 31 (1961)
Section Representative:
Priscilla Llewelyn (Rickard)

Sarah Bays (Fisher) We have had a couple of trips abroad and in July, as a belated seventy-fifth birthday celebration, we are taking the whole family to Greece. I play a bit of bridge and am otherwise enjoying our five delightful grandchildren.

On a sad note, in the Autumn John and I went to a Memorial Service for **Judy Evans (Beesley)**. The church was packed – she was much loved. **Sue Nock (Constance)**, **Jill Selkirk (Churcher)**, **Tricia Rudland (Hopkins)** and **Primrose (Moran)** were also there.

Vanessa Cook (Hall) Really the news never changes! Now have two great grandchildren but luckily am fit after two new knees and still running the garden and nursery. Anyone managing to reach Yorkshire would be very welcome. We have a very good café!

Sue Garden (The Rt Hon the Baroness Garden of Frognal) (Button) No great changes. Still a deputy speaker and Liberal Democrat remit for universities, colleges, skills and apprenticeships and still horrified by Brexit! Great family visit to New York, World Traders visit to Dublin and Edinburgh Festival with my sister Patricia. Daughter Alex still Chief Exec of Hampshire NHS Trust, daughter Antonia primary teacher in London. Eldest grandson, Henry, at Glasgow University. How the years fly by!

Priscilla Llewelyn (Rickard) First, I would like to send my sympathies on behalf of our section, to the families of **Caroline Boswell** and **Judy Evans (Beesley)** who have died this year.

May I also say a big thank you to everyone who has sent their news in - it's really lovely to have it. Now here goes - my news:

Seventy-five years have been and gone last August, with hardly a ripple. I was still running the Residential Home and enjoying it. However, after nearly thirty-two years I started thinking about its future and decided it was better to leave while the going was good. So, in November, I sold it on to my son, Hugo, and he, and now his three siblings, are involved there and doing a good job. Nowadays it's all about regulation, which I was never very happy with; I, with others, were so lucky to start up in 1987 when it was much more like looking after a large family.

So, at Hugo's suggestion I enrolled for part-time study at Cardiff University and am absolutely loving it! This term is Creative Writing and next term Major Events in Welsh History. It's really odd how good it is to study now and yet how horrid I found history at Westonbirt. However, I notice from my grandchildren's reports that, thank goodness, the subject is much more interesting these days.

I have nine grandchildren, who are great fun. I don't see enough of them but at least I'm lucky that we all live in the same country.

I'm in the process of moving to a house that I have renovated in the village of Llanvihangel Crucorney. It's far too large for one, but it does mean that I have spare bedrooms available for any OG's who might be in the area - on the Hereford side of Abergavenny and still in the Brecon Beacons National Park. Please get in touch if you are anywhere near - I'd love to see you!

With best wishes to everyone and have a good year.

Jane Merritt (Wilkinson) This has been another eventful year. In April we went to Keith's fiftieth reunion since his graduation from the US Military Academy at West Point. It was a busy, four-day celebration with full military parade, banquets, etc. It was my first visit there, and I was very impressed with the beauty of the surrounding country and of course with the buildings themselves.

Earlier in March, we spent a week in Waikiki Beach, Hawaii with my step-sister Sally Anne and her husband from Sydney, Australia. It was wonderful to see her again. In August, I was in Denmark to visit Michael and the family. This time we spent some time on the Island of Bornholm, which is beautiful. It was great to catch up with my extended family there and to practice speaking Danish again!

At church, I am still very involved in the daily activities and serve at the altar at the midweek Eucharist services. Keith and I are very active, holding worship services in two prisons in the region.

I still get out and run about five miles most mornings at the crack of dawn. Each year my pace is slower, but I enjoy the exercise and it is a wonderful start to the day. I listen to sermons and other related podcasts as I run. I especially enjoy the ones from the UK (St Paul's Cathedral, St. Martin's in the Field).

Michael is still at Microsoft and enjoying life with the family. He broke his arm skiing last month, but otherwise the family is well. I look forward to catching up on the Westonbirt news later.

Sue Patchett (Greenwood) Not much news from Sydney. As far as old girls go - I heard from **Rosie Edgington** that **Caroline Boswell** died very suddenly last year. I saw both Rosie and **Felicity Napier** last year while in UK visiting my sister Caroline Shelford and the family.

Australia, as most other countries, is suffering from climate change and the floods in the north and fires in general are becoming fiercer and fiercer. I witnessed a controlled burn on our property a few years ago now and the intensity and implosion of heat really made me realise how devastating these fires are.

On a more cheerful note, the grandchildren are still a huge source of joy even though Charlotte is fourteen and looking twenty - as they do!

Best wishes to all and sundry.

Angela Sellings (Marson) We have now been in our new home for eighteen months and have finally got it sorted so we are happy with everything. We had the garden (very small) landscaped last year so I can now look forward to no mowing and mostly pots to look after. We enjoyed the lovely weather last summer as we had no lawn to worry about and could enjoy sitting outside on the new patio. We have just returned from a couple of weeks staying with friends in Cape Town which was a real treat. Life at home carries on much the same with walking with friends and weekly classes of Pilates and Qi Gong keeping the body from seizing up. I also doing volunteer driving to take people to doctors, hospitals and dentists.

Gillian Wynes (Ross Goobey) I had a lovely visit from my son Anthony, my daughter-in-law Jenny, and grandchildren George and Millie from America in August last year. We went out for the day, and then the rest of the family joined us, and we all went out for a meal in the evening. It was super seeing them all.

We had an excellent time on Christmas Day. We went to my daughter Deborah's house, where we had a wonderful lunch and played silly games afterwards.

Section 30 (1960)
Section Representative:
Jane Reid (Bottomley)

It was likely that there would be an informal get-together in the summer of 2019 as suggested by **Jean Astill** (see below) – some had expressed interest, and a location (Holland Park Cafeteria) had been suggested. All that was needed was a date – and perhaps an organiser!

Carolyn Reynolds (Mathison) and **Barbara Workman (May)** had been in contact during the year.

Ann Beard (Harverson), **Penelope Cowell (Bowring)**, **Lesley Godwin (Neil)**, **Joan Madonko (Scott)**, **Jill McEwan (Montgomerie)**, **Jane Palestrini (Drew)**, **Juliet Peel (de Galleani)**, **Sallie Sullivan (Sanderson***)* had acknowledged mailings.

Phoebe Field (Northcroft), **Janet Kingston (Oakeley)**, **Jane Reid (Bottomley)**, **Rosemary Somers (Fuchs-Marx)** attended the Association AGM in 2018

When **Jean Astill (MacKenzie)** emailed, she was unsure whether she would make the AGM but felt that another contemporaries' low-key meeting in London would be great fun if anyone was feeling strong enough to organise it.

Bodhiniya (Ann Udal) was just moving to a flat in a sheltered complex when she emailed in mid-February. She felt lucky, because it had two bedrooms. It was run by a housing association in an old converted house, with a portico with two lions sitting on it! The flat needed stuff done to it, but she thought that it would suit her well. It was in Moseley where she was already living, and near two of her daughters and the Buddhist centre she was part of.

Phoebe Field (Northcroft) had had two trips back to UK in 2018, which had enabled a catch-up with the families and an interesting visit with her sisters to Westonbirt in May. They lost their sister-in-law in July, which took some adjusting to. The grandchildren grew apace, with number one having started school in February. They were ever a source of laughter. A growthy spring had given way to a warm summer, but the trees had had a good drink after the dry years. All was well otherwise.

Jane Reid (Bottomley) continued to do very little of note, but found herself busy far too often, particularly as the condition of the house and garden just got worse each year because of the lack of time. Otherwise, all was well.

Anne Rennie (McCullagh) had a lovely reunion with **Lesley Godwin (Neill)** in Sydney before Christmas. Anne had been one of Lesley's bridesmaids. It did them both good to catch up with their past and share stories about their different lives. Lesley had moved to Canada and Anne to Australia after their respective marriages; they both understood the feeling of having one foot in one country and one in another. The reunion had been a good time with lots to talk about.

Rosemary Somers (Fuchs-Marx) emailed that there was good news – Tony was in full remission from both his cancers – and bad news – Rosemary had been diagnosed with Parkinson's: her hands trembled, she tired quickly, and she had become clumsier and stiff legged. She commented that trembling does not hurt or kill, and she had found that it seemed to use up extra calories, so she no longer needed to watch her weight. She was faithfully following a course of physiotherapy to strengthen muscles and maintain balance. Tony did weekly yoga, Rosemary, Zumba, and both continued with tennis.

She said that that was enough of her 'organ recital' and moved on to the many trips out that they had made during the year – some in London such as Wimbledon and the Lord Mayor's Show, some further afield on their own (including Westonbirt in May) or with family. The major trip, to the USA, was based around the triennial Fuchs family reunion, this time in California with seventy attending.

To Rosemary and Tony's delight, no construction having yet taken place on the site of the former Earls Court Exhibition Centre at the bottom of their garden, they experienced a second winter with sun in the house. They continued to feel blessed that they lived close enough to their children and grandchildren to see them frequently. All were thriving.

Bridget Towle emailed that life continued; at the end of July she would complete her term of office as the Chair of Council of the University of Leicester. She had much enjoyed her association with the university, though amazed and amused that after a non-academic school career such a link had occurred.

Section 29 (1959)
Section Representative:
Myrth Russell (Hudson)

Nonie Beckinsale News from Newcastle Emlyn: The major event of the year was probably my husband Mike's eightieth birthday. We celebrated with a large tea party in the local community hall for lots of the people locally whom we work with and see day to day as well as a number of very old and dear friends. All our family managed to get down for the event and helped with the setting up and clearing away afterwards.

Speaking of family, at the end of the summer, only one of the grandchildren will be still at school. Sam is back from his splendid two years in Canada and looking for a paramedics course; Ben is coming to the end of his BBC traineeship; Joe is training with the Welsh Cycle Team; Barney is working in a school specialising in hard-to-teach children; Jake is doing A Levels – and that leaves just Annie!

We managed a little holiday in September on the Italian Riviera – lovely coastline and lots of fishy food. Otherwise we are pretty busy here, keeping the house and garden in order, running the church choir, looking after the PCC, Mothers' Union, British Legion etc.

Sue Bowden (Humpidge) We still live quietly in our little woodland cottage. Lambing only a dozen ewes this year but we still have a LOT of rare breed chickens - a very good occupation for retired clergyman…We enjoy taking the donkey and other animals around to various schools, churches and care homes and are honoured to take part every Palm Sunday at Gloucester Cathedral with them.

Our eight grandchildren are a real joy and both families live within an hour away. Baby Claudia is our greatest blessing - after the tragedy of Bonnie,s death two years ago.

It's increasingly special to get together with old friends from school, now that we are so old…! And **Libby Houston, Lin Hutton, Caroline Price** and l keep in close touch (even had a day at the races together!) Always love to see other old girls too.

Some of our grandchildren do Tetrathlon At Westonbirt, including cross-country running. Brings back memories of that run to the main gate every morning before breakfast…

Helen Brown We are still here in Cumbria on our smallholding and about to start lambing again, though we are cutting down on our flock of rare-breed sheep.

I do hope you manage to get relief from your sciatica, it is such a nasty thing. My artificial joints (two knees and an ankle) have been a blessing, I can walk five miles without pain and hope to manage one or two easier Lake District fells this summer.

We are about to go off to Portugal for a much-needed week's break. We had to abandon plans for a big holiday to Australia as Philip fell and fractured a bone in his spine. Fortunately, he has recovered well, but it is a reminder that we are not as young as we used to be.

Lin Coleman My news doesn't seem to change from one year to the next, but as I can't remember what I wrote last year, here goes:

I'm still working part-time as a psychotherapist for individuals and couples. It's challenging but rewarding work, and as it's a second career I am still enthusiastic and continually learning.

Gardening, Tai Chi and doing patchwork keep me occupied, and I also love singing in a London vocal jazz choir, that I joined over fifteen years ago (Google 'Take 20'). The group has been going for forty years this year and there were just over twenty people when I joined, but we're now just over thirty. The arrangements are in-house and jazz chords are not the same as the classical chords engrained in me so well at Westonbirt, but it's such fun.

I have to have an 'Italy fix' every year, but apart from that am very content at home.

Libby Houston Still at work in the Avon Gorge, mostly checking on the populations of the extraordinary number of rare and important plants, from tiny (sometimes only 1cm high) early annual cress, Hutchinsia, to the eighteen Whitebeam tree species (five of which evolved in the Gorge and grow nowhere else in the world), and clearing and killing invasive aliens like cotoneaster and holm oak that can quickly destroy the open cliff habitats – and leading walks, and answering queries. Last autumn I was part of a roped team clearing soil from the Suspension Bridge cliff ledges with shovels for a geological survey! I was also extremely honoured to receive the Marsh Botany Award for 2018, from the Marsh Christian Trust, an amazing charity that recognises work in all kinds of fields. Back in the normal world, I visited my son and his family in New Zealand, where we stayed in a nature reserve and had a day cutting back very different vegetation! Had some lovely days with **Caroline Sturdy** (**Price**) and **Sue Bowden** (**Humpidge**), and *may* manage to visit **Jennifer Scully** (**Parker**) in Toronto this year...

Linda Morley Last year was not the best of years. Sadly, my sister-in-law died in the summer after a protracted illness. However, my sister Phoebe came over twice from New Zealand which was a bonus. We drove up to Scotland to visit our cousin and Phe's friends which was enjoyable. I went on a short trip to France with my partner in May. Choral Society activities took up some time and we once again provided the anthem at the St George's Day Service in Gloucester Cathedral, this year attended by Princess Anne.

I had a memorable visit to Kos with the European Union of Women in late September. Representatives from seven countries attended and we once again discussed the refugee problems in Europe. I went into an extinct (for now) volcano crater, which was fun, on the island of Nissyros. The highlight for me was the declamation of the Hippocratic Oath, in ancient Greek, and repeated in modern Greek, at the site of the Asklipeion temple and the Hippocratic Museum, which had been arranged for us by one of the Greek members. This was stunning and most memorable in such an authentic setting. It was great to be reunited with so many friends from different countries.

In August I found myself with two three-month-old puppies. What terrible rascals they were, destroying everything in sight - litter sisters, half Dachshund and half Yorkshire Terrier, very pretty girls! They have at last quietened down and provide me with endless walks. Now just awaiting all the Brexit results, having spent too much time watching proceedings in Parliament - straight from the horses' mouths. A short trip to Madeira soon might calm me down!

Myrth Russel We, with our dog Molly, are still in Helensburgh, alongside the Clyde Estuary. In June we spent a couple of weeks in Tuscany. We, like many Brits, get olive oil and other stuff from the farm La Vialle, so we had decided to visit this farm of smiling and warmly welcoming hosts. The tiny old cottage we had chosen was high in the hills, and beautifully accoutered. The villages in the Tuscan hills charmed us, so that we must return. This is not so easy as I am suddenly blighted with lower back trouble which prevents me from walking, except from pottering about, bent over, around the house. Luckily, I can sit comfortably, and so playing the violin, and bridge, is fine. I will have seen the consultant about possible operations by the time this is received. We are just about to plant potatoes for our neighbourly competition; five potatoes in a bag. So far, we have not won! With luck I may soon be restored to uprightness, and we might win with the potatoes.

Eileen Stewardson 2018 was a horrendous year for us. Mike had a coronary (fortunately small) just after Christmas 2017. Then at the end of June a cotton tunic I was wearing caught fire in a candle flame. I have to recommend the emergency services and the response to our frantic 999 call, as in minutes a paramedic ambulance and fire appliance had arrived at the house. Poor Mike burnt his hands tearing the wretched garment off. As it caught fire from the back, I couldn't see what was going on, just feel it. Fortunately, there is a specialist burns unit in Bristol who were super. The plus to all this is that I spent some of the hottest days last summer in an air-conditioned room. **Linda Morley**, bless her, came down to see me.

Also, a plus was that my daughter, Sian, was able to come over from Australia to help us after we finally got home. It was an extreme way of seeing friends and family, which I do not recommend.

Otherwise life is much as usual.

Section 28 (1958)
Section Representative:
Sue Hicks (Harker)

Thanks to all four who replied this year. A special mention is due to **Anne Mercer** for her interesting account of their visit to Israel. However even if you have done 'nothing' all year, we are still delighted to hear from you, however briefly.

Sheila Astbury (Stuart) It was good to meet up with **Sue Hicks**, **Val Sill** and **Anne Mercer** at the AGM last year and to see other friends from the distant past.

The grandchildren are a delight and I am lucky to see them regularly. Last year holidays took me to southern Greece and also to the Sierra Nevada mountains in southern Spain when the summer heat was over.

Sue Hicks (Harker) We enjoyed the AGM at Westonbirt last May too. We had two Italian holidays last year, both of which were most enjoyable. The first was in Rome, where we spent a week with my brother and partner from New Zealand, following their Mediterranean Cruise.

We saw an excellent performance of *La Traviata* while we were there. In Florence, later in the year, we saw *The Barber of Seville* sung brilliantly by a small group in a church.

Vet daughter Rosemary is also an accomplished athlete and mother of four boys, while Jacqueline continues to juggle a tree surgery business, taxi service, teenage daughters, music and aging parents. My husband, John, had a week in hospital in the summer with a mystery fever, but is fine now. I still attend various U3A groups and enjoy gardening.

Anne Mercer (Seear) Suffice to say that other than celebrating the school's ninetieth birthday celebrations with **Sheila Astbury**, **Sue Hicks** and Valerie Sill, while the two husbands went to the Arboretum, the highlight of our year was last August/September when Bill and I enjoyed a ten-day pilgrimage to Israel with a small group (twenty-three) of all but two from our parish church and the four benefice villages.

It was arranged literally door-to-door which made it very simple. We stayed in Jerusalem for six nights in the Golden Walls Hotel between Herod's Gate and Damascus Gate so enjoyed wandering around the city after dinner. The days were long and exhausting with almost too much packed into each, at least for first-time pilgrims like ourselves. Our first day was to the Mount of Olives with panoramic views of the walled city, visiting Pater Noster church, where supposedly Jesus gave the Lord's Prayer to his disciples, and Dominus Flevit Chapel, in the garden of which we were stunned by the length and viciousness of the thorns used to make the crown which was crammed on to Jesus' head. We then walked down the very steep hill which Jesus must have used frequently walking from Bethany to Jerusalem, to the Church of All Nations in the Garden of Gethsemane, continuing after lunch to the Israel Museum to see the stunning model of ancient Jerusalem and the Dead Sea Scrolls.

The next day we crossed into Palestinian territory to visit Bethlehem and the Fields of the Shepherds, lunching at the Bethlehem Rehabilitation Centre and hearing about their work before entering Manger Square and visiting the Basilica and Grotto of the Nativity as well as St Jerome's caves.

Then we made the long drive through the Judean wilderness to Qumran to explore the well-preserved site near where the Dead Sea Scrolls were discovered, and on to Herod's desert fortress Masada, ascending by cable car. After lunch we floated in the horribly salty and slimy and diminishing Dead Sea. Our final call was to Wadi Qelt for wonderful views of St George's Monastery.

Our Sunday was less full, with a very early morning visit to the church of the Holy Sepulchre, where all was peace and quiet, to witness the variety of liturgies, followed by joining the local congregation at St George's Cathedral, lunch and an afternoon visit to grim Yad Vasham Memorial to the holocaust.

Our final day in Jerusalem was formally entering the Old City through Zion Gate, walking through the Jewish quarter to the Western Wall and on to Temple Mount with the El Aqsa Mosque and dome of the Rock, ending by the Pool of Bethesda and following the Via Dolorosa to the church of the Holy Sepulchre.

We then left Jerusalem, driving first to Bethany, briefly visiting the tomb of Lazarus, continuing to the desert oasis of Jericho, viewing the Mount of Temptation, before heading north to Galilee. We stopped *en route* at the Jordan River valley baptismal sight which was another disappointment because the river was no wider than the narrow river Great Ouse which meanders through our market town here in Buckingham.

From our hotel in Tiberius our coach navigated the winding road to reach the beautiful Basilica of the Transfiguration with its magnificent views over the plain of Armageddon and then to Nazareth. In the afternoon we walked to Mary's Well, returning to Tiberius via Cana, the scene of Jesus' first miracle.

On our penultimate day we visited sites associated with Jesus' life around the shrinking Sea of Galilee, beginning with Capernaum and continuing to Mensa Christa, where Jesus appeared to His disciples after His resurrection, celebrating (one of many) Holy Communion services at Tabgha, right beside the Sea of Galilee, and visiting the Church of the Loaves and Fishes. We lunched at the convent of the Beatitudes with a visit to the church and garden commemorating the Sermon on the Mount, finally walking down to the lake and sailing back across the calm Sea of Galilee to our hotel.

Our last day saw us leaving Tiberius and driving to the Mediterranean coast and the Roman capital of Caesarea where we visited the restored amphitheatre and amazing aqueduct before flying home.

Margaret Squires (Renshaw) My life is very samey. More mountains. We thought we had finally collected all the Marilyns* we could do (i.e. all except the St. Kilda Sea Stacks) and hit number 1551/1556 on Usinis in a wild part of the island of Lewis in June. Then the surveyors measured another one in the wilds of the Cape Wrath peninsula. We may have a shot at it, but with Roger's knee deteriorating year by year, we won't be able to do it between the first and last tourist bus to the lighthouse, so may have to camp. Now starting on the Wainwrights in the Lakes. I still swim most days I don't get a good walk in. Eldest grandson graduated from St Andrews, where he was staying with us, and is now at University in Paris; in fact, they are all (four) at various stages in their education. Met up with **Janet Gregory** for the first time since we were both at different universities in the early sixties. It was great to catch up with her.

*Hills with a 150m drop between them and the next one ie from Ben Nevis down.

Catherine Whittingham (Norman Moses) We are in Portugal for a month (written in March 2019) escaping the Canadian winter. No news except we are reasonably well and there's nothing too much to report, which is good at our age. Our dearly loved grandchild who we have raised from a baby has fled the nest to university, so we miss her hugely, but quiet life is fine.

Sections 26 & 27 (1956 and 1957)
Section Representative:
Angela Potter (Tracy)

After a bit of pestering I'm pleased to be able to provide sixteen correspondents, from my two sections, for the WB News. Most of us are now eighty or thereabouts, so there is not really much excitement to write about!

Personally, I am glad to report that all is well in the Potter household (no significant age-related problems) and we carry on much as we have done for the last fifty-five years. Long may it last. An African safari is planned for October! Our four children are gainfully employed, and our grandchildren (all ten of them) growing up to be useful citizens, the four eldest already at university.

Living in Westonbirt – the very last place I expected to be in my later years - we are still very much involved with the school and the Arboretum! I with the history of the Holford family and with the Trust that is trying to raise money to restore the historic fabric of the house and garden, and Malcolm as a guide at the Arboretum. He has found a totally new passion for trees, including those in Westonbirt garden.

There were twelve of us in my Dorchester year group, and I have the email addresses of all but one (apart of course from dear **Sue Powell (Watkins)** who died a few years ago). Please contact me through the school if you would like to find any past friends. I understand that **Pauline Hathorn (Horrocks)** and **Helen Lilley (Blakeborough)**, Joan's sister, are both suffering from dementia. Helen is still living on her own – just.

Section 27

Joan Allan (Blakeborough) Not much news this last year. The highlight was seventeen days in Chile in November. We left there in June 1980 and met again some people whom we had not seen for thirty-eight years! We were made very welcome. We found Santiago unrecognisable - wonderful infrastructure now, and so modern. We went down to the coast and visited our beloved Juana in Zapallar - now ninety, and still as clear as a bell and seemingly unaltered since we last saw her some years ago. A wonderful reunion but so sad to say a final goodbye.

We also stayed with a naval friend in Viña. Spring in Chile is so lovely with all the flowering trees and bushes, as well as the flowers. Venezuela is now what Chile would have become but for the timely intervention of their armed forces and General Pinochet.

It has been a good year for our sons. Our eldest, Hugo, is very happy with the legal partnership he changed to three years ago and was elected to the Executive Council in the autumn. Our second son, Nick, was made CEO of Control Risks, the global security firm he has worked with for many years. Our youngest, Colin, is being posted from Azerbaijan to Trinidad next August which excites us - and them - greatly. Alexandra's family made a fortune there and she thinks there are still relatives surviving in the area. We hope to visit!

Our grandchildren mostly thrive. The family all visit us once a year and then we have an annual Scottish family reunion, sadly missed last year. This year we are having a week all together near Lochinver at the end of July. We struggle along, getting slower and with parts of us not working as they did, but so far, we are extremely fortunate. I still play golf once a week with aged friends as bad as me, and we continue with our social duplicate bridge. I also play duplicate bridge at the Golf Club when l can.

Judith Briggs (Walker) Still living in our townhouse in Parktown North, Johannesburg, with Peter, and we are able to keep reasonably active. We started last year with all the family together over Christmas in the Cape and were able to continue with our visits to the Game Reserve area in South Africa which we much enjoy. It was a quiet year for us as I had to have a knee replacement, but that went well, and I can now do most everything normally once again.

We were able to travel to the United States to visit the family there (Alexandra, our doctor daughter, lives just outside Boston) so could catch up with the US teenagers, Claire now seventeen and Max and Charlie, fifteen, all at high school, and doing OK. We stopped over in London on the way home to see my sister Annie but missed sister Sue who lives in Tasmania by a few days, unfortunately.

We went to the Cape again in December to catch up with Guy (twin brother of Alex) and that family - Anna, thirteen and just off to senior school, and Oliver, ten, at a close-by prep school.

We were hardly back when we went off again, this time to join a group going to Norway for a trip on one of the Hurtigruten ferries which ply up and down the Norwegian west costs, along the fjords and up into the Arctic Circle - quite magical, and good Northern Lights viewing, though much more muted colours than one is lead to expect from the bright colour photos - but beautiful just the same.

So, we chug along - am still involved in various aspects of the local community, including the political scene, which has improved, but from such a low base that anything other than that the previous incumbent would seem good! Continued exposure of the corruption that occurred under the previous lot, and which we hope has been curtailed, but the prosecutions that are needed are a long time coming. Now in the throes of an election campaign - the outcome is likely to be interesting!

Priscilla Boddington (Pentreath) I spent some time last year living with a daughter while I found a new home nearer to my family than the lovely village of Crowcombe where I had lived for over twenty years. I have now moved into a small terrace house in Hungerford within easy reach of all the many local facilities. Although I very much regret leaving Somerset, I am sure I have made the right move. I very much enjoy being more central to my family - all the three generations - but I do miss my Somerset friends! Just home from the funeral in Dorset of my brother's wife - the gathering of so many members of our extensive family is very reassuring despite the sadness of the reason we were meeting on this occasion.

Gillie Drake (Strain) Not a lot to report, only that we shall soon be the proud possessors of some Silver Sebrights (chickens) which will include staying with **Priscilla Boddington** in her new home in Hungerford. Looking forward to that.

Christabel Cumberlege (Jaques) We are both hale and hearty, (I am heartily grateful that I can still write 'we') and Mike is still able to mow the lawns and do the washing-up! Our sons and their families are much more exciting, running, swimming, cycling and turning these skills into triathlons last year at Hever Castle in Kent where it poured with rain.

This year we are all going to stay with elder son Dominic and his wife Lesley who have an olive grove in Tuscany near Cortona so there will be us and also Tom, Sophie and their three children, Rupert (10), Ralph (7) and Alice (4). (The latter family still live in Upper Norwood).

If that might be a bit tiring, we will be travelling along the Danube on a river boat in September. We have never been to Mittel Europe before. Otherwise we waste an awful lot of time reading and watching news on Brexit and hope we don't hope in vain for a satisfactory resolution. Perhaps Paddy Ashdown has chosen a wise time to depart this life, so much missed in our lovely village. He had a marvellous send-off, everyone turned out to be part of his funeral.

Rowena Ginns (Cullin) 2018 was not a good year for us health-wise, I had a nasty throat operation and Bill a spinal op that afforded no improvement. After a long recovery I am now alright. We did manage a Rhine Cruise which was very enjoyable and some of the usual coaching activities.

The family continue to thrive, and the London flat affords us the opportunity to meet up. James is still with Cathay Pacific and still lives in Richmond, and his eldest son Andrew who graduated with a Masters in IT is job-seeking in London, Harry is at Bristol University, Sam is about to read Classics at Cambridge, and Thomas is back in Hong Kong at school. Jonathan continues to spend his time circumnavigating the world as a Lawyer with INEOS. His three sons are younger and all doing well at school. This year we hope to have our usual ten days at Royal Ascot, to drive our horses at Sandringham and at Flores Castle, and to compete at Windsor, Suffolk and Newbury Shows, fingers crossed!

Alison Reed (Hill) Life continues much the same. Anthony's dementia has its ups and downs. But I manage to get reasonable help. I still play golf. I recently had my eightieth birthday - hard to believe! And it is amazing to still be in close touch with several Westonbirt friends; one advantage of being in London. I do miss getting to Northumberland on a regular basis - although I have managed the occasional weekend, which has been a real tonic.

Rhonnie Watts (Murray) It has been a difficult year as I developed diabetes, Getting old! Otherwise busy with the family and playing golf. Am spending a lot of time at Hayling Island which I enjoy, and the lifestyle down here. Hope to get down to the school some time before too long!

Section 26

Felicity Coultard (Scott) Last year I decided to do a bit of travelling. I went to Holland twice, to Italy once and round Ireland on a cruise ship. Holland on a river boat with my blind friend was good. Italy alone but in a group was excellent, we stayed in the Italian version of Harrogate and explored the area. The highlight was a castle where we had a cookery demonstration followed by a five-course dinner with one of their own wines with each course. I did not take kindly to cruising, though my blind friend coped with it well. Far too many people on thirteen decks. I don't intend to go abroad again. Airports are awful. Holidays this year will be in Britain. Otherwise I am happily settled in my home of fifty-two years with family next door and plenty to occupy me. I'm ever more arthritic and have given up gardening. But I can still drive and that is what matters.

Jane Hancock (Quale) My husband, David, and myself are very fortunate in that we are reasonably fit and able. We are travelling as much as we can while we can! We have been on several lovely cruises during the year. The last two of these were in the Caribbean where we enjoyed lovely sunny days while Britain was cold. We are due to go to Buenos Aires in April to cruise up the coast of Brazil and then across the Atlantic to Barcelona stopping at a lot of interesting places on the way. Our children and grandchildren are mostly fit and flourishing. Chloe, our youngest granddaughter (nearly 5), is in remission from her cancer and we can only pray that it will not return. She has started at nursey school but is still not too steady when walking or running. Best wishes to everyone.

Margaret Jackson (Grubb) Absolutely nothing of note to report. I am well, taking no medication, which I am told is rare for my age – my main query is how did I get to be this age anyway?! We went on a very pleasant river cruise up the Rhine and Moselle last year. This year we are off at the beginning of April cruising up the West coast of England to Stornoway, then back via Dublin and the Scilly Isles. We call at a few other places too. I simply wanted to be out of the reach of any family 'fuss' for my eightieth birthday. (I think I am a year behind many of my section!) As we are both in good health we have optimistically booked a cruise – Kiel Canal to Gdansk – starting at the end of September 2020, when, all being well, we shall just have celebrated our diamond wedding. Our three offspring are all in their fifties – that's a shock in itself. Our eldest grandchild is getting married this summer. Life goes on, despite B****t.

Valerie Mitchell (Noad) We're still in our lovely home and plan changes to our en-suite bathroom. I've survived two total-knee replacements (mostly successful), left eye cataract (successful) and carpal tunnel syndrome (not). Our village Shop is still going, run by volunteers, but after ten years, I am "retiring" from duties, though Anthony continues - thankfully some new arrivals are joining the rota. Daughter Suzanne bought a retired polo pony, and we enjoy watching her play when we holiday in Edinburgh. We love seeing Philippa and family who now live in Surrey; she is home-educating Leila (10) and Jamie (6) - very different, and I'm amazed at how many brave mums do this, with more facilities available during the day for these children. Anthony and I are enjoying sorting out our many cine films of our life and work in Botswana, Malawi, Tanzania, Kenya and England, getting them made into longer reels so that our daughters are reminded of their early life!

Rachel Palmer (Phillips) A brief brief: I recommend Penelope Lively's *Ammonites and Flying Fish* to all of those celebrating the big 8-0. The bit on what books are worth rereading is especially interesting. My three eldest grandchildren are working in London now and it is a joy to see them from time to time. Each has a career brief to be challenged by, enjoy and work hard at, but it all concerns worlds which I struggle to understand. The three-year sponsored fellowship in memory of my son Stephen is progressing with research at Cambridge into schizophrenia, it is administered by the newish mental health research charity MQ (www.mqmentalhealth.org). Along with **Diana Ashby** and *Fiona Holland* I have been left a small legacy by a TCD (Trinity College Dublin) friend to finance a get-together which is a very pleasant and unexpected surprise. We are booked to go to Dublin for three nights in August. I came to Tetbury last year for Jennifer's eightieth and got snowed in!

Cyrilla Potter (Monk) It is more than a year now since my beloved Roy died. After twenty-nine happy years together, he is sorely missed. Last October I travelled abroad for the first time in eight years, to Sorrento with my grandson Alister. It was lovely to go back and be remembered by so many people there.

I visited old friends in Leicester in December and flew to New York for Christmas and New Year, staying with my daughter Catherine and her husband Hugh at their beautiful house on Long Island. It was two days after my seventy-ninth birthday when I set off for my very first visit to the USA. An amazing experience flying there on my own. I felt very intrepid.

On 1st March this crazy woman is flying out to New York again and when I return my daughter will be coming with me for meetings in London and Oxford. **Veronica Graham Brown (Howarth)** and I keep in touch. She has just returned from a wonderful trip to Kuala Lumpur and Hong Kong. I enjoy writing poetry and am writing a book about my life so some of the questions people wish they had asked you sooner will be answered.

Anne Renard (Matthews) I hope that no-one is, like me, enmeshed in a cocoon of care, having tripped and fallen in the kitchen, and broken my femur. I was in hospital for surgery on my leg, and now I'm in a nursing care home, confined to the bed or chair, as I'm not allowed to put any weight on my leg at the moment. I'm currently trying to keep in shape by working out how to keep a day's worth of activities and necessities within reach, even with a long-handled grabber! At least now, I'm back in a stable routine with my Parkinson's medications, having suffered a few days in hospital from the disruptions to my usual schedule mixed with a cocktail of painkillers and anaesthetic. Best wishes and good health to all.

Oriel Rogers-Coltman (Corbett) Our life in Shropshire continues much as before. Having resolved not to get too involved in "events" after we moved, I foolishly suggested that Lydbury North should resurrect their Open Gardens weekend. With lots of help we managed to have a successful two days in June and made over £2,000 for the church roof fund. (A very small contribution towards the £200,000 that will be needed!) I do my weekly shift behind the village shop counter – luckily there is a good till because arithmetic has never been my strong suit. Otherwise there are often grandchildren to be ferried here and there but because we enjoy being near them so much it's a small price to pay. We went to the Italian Lakes last May and saw some lovely gardens and villas.

Section 25 (1955)
Section Representative:
Jill Gibson (Connor)

Once again, I thank those of you who responded so swiftly to my request for news – it's good to keep in touch but I think the time has come for me to hand over as section rep to someone else. So, if any of you would be willing to take on the collection of news, etc I would love to hear from you.

Elisabeth Abrahams (Langford) told me in a phone call that she was still 'jogging along' – thankfully she is still driving so able to get out and about to local activities. Her grandchildren give her great enjoyment. She is in touch with **Lynn Levy**.

Beth Barrington Haynes celebrated her eightieth birthday with a superb river cruise, Strasbourg to Amsterdam, enjoying the luxury of a butler while on board! And she gave a party at the Hurlingham Club to celebrate the occasion as well. She has met up with **Tatiana Eyre** (now **Hurd**), **Alyn (Paisley)** and sees **Bridget Frost (Kell)** who is also living at Rivermead Court.

Bridget Frost (Kell) wrote on her return from Thailand, in a year where she has done much travelling. She and her sisters have been sorting out her mothers' affairs and belongings. She too celebrated her eightieth birthday with a party at the Hurlingham Club where **Heather Owen (Grange)** and **Rosemary Kitson (Hines)** joined her as well as **Beth**.

Jill Gibson (Connor) The same activities as usual keep me out of mischief and Ken still manages two rounds of golf a week. Douglas, now a brigadier, is presently stationed in Ramallah on the West Bank and we hope to visit him, combining this with a trip to the Red Sea for some snorkelling, maybe in September. Everyone else is doing the same things as last year.

Patricia Hedges' (Crow) main news is the publishing of her book about her mother's amazing life, *The Raj, the Rolls and the Remorse*. This can be obtained on Amazon or by e-mailing Patricia. (You can contact her through her section rep or the school). Hope it's a hit – I'm sure it deserves to be.

Veronica Graham Brown has also been travelling – a cruise from Singapore to Hong Kong with time both there and in Kuala Lumpur. The eightieth birthday party in Scotland she was planning last year took place in a house on the shores of Loch Tay with a big family gathering. She keeps in touch with **Cyrilla Potter**.

Lynn Levy (Drapkin) has moved to Erskine Hill. You can contact her through her section rep or the school. She and her husband are very thankful that they are still able to travel but not long-haul anymore. This year's special event will be a week in Crete with all her far-flung family there except one granddaughter who is studying in Hong Kong. Her sister **Caryl** still struggles on but with very little memory left.

Section 24 (1954)
Section Representative:
Alison Robinson (De Courcy-Ireland)

Sadly, fewer replies this year – hardly surprising since we are mostly, if not all, into our ninth decade. But, as always, my gratitude to those who have replied and who all seem to be keeping mentally active, even if more limited physically.

Elizabeth Bennett (Anning) says she is still alive. She doesn't moan about what she can't do, just enjoys what she can. An active UAE keeps her occupied and, she says, although she now has type 2 diabetes, she can still feel able to murder a pack of crisps but is able to sit and look at a slice of chocolate cake!

Elizabeth Ells (Rawlence) feels lucky to still be physically well and active. She is more and more interested in photography and in September went for a ten-day photographic expedition to Iceland, which was incredibly interesting *(and she sent her Section Rep an amazing photograph she had taken of a clear iceberg)*. She adds: "We have had a brutal winter, almost three metres of snow already, 2 March, and daytime high temperatures are mostly well below freezing since Christmas. It was such fun to revisit Westonbirt for the Old Girls/Open House day last March, so many changes, so much the same!"

Amelia Gardner (Langford) is still "ticking along"' with the help of her able carer, shopper and chauffeur: husband Ian, who will be eighty-five next month. Amelia hasn't been out of Pembrokeshire for a year and a half since having a bleed on the brain but has had a nice lot of family visitors who enjoy being so near the sea and the house has proved unexpectedly adaptable. They are now looking forward to the arrival of the Abuan Bible which Ian has been working on for many years. It has been typeset in Switzerland, printed in Korea and should soon be on the high seas en route to Nigeria, where its launching is eagerly anticipated.

Caryll Green's **(Rees-Reynolds)** life revolves around gardening, golf, travel and of course family. She finished a three-year stint on the parish council last May, which was rewarding, but time-consuming. Caryll had seen **Rosemary Kitson (Hines)** who was in good spirits but has some health issues.

Sheena Mackenzie also says she's still here, bit bored, just playing competitive bridge, and enjoying friendships within her condo building, which has the advantage that "one can have some wine and only drive the elevator home. We have now all made it a point of not doing dinner, just drinks and nibbles, which means we partake more often." Cannabis use has been made legal in Canada, but Sheena says, "it makes no difference to me!"

Valerie Moorby's **(Holmes-Johnson)** most important piece of news was the acquisition of a great-grandson in May last year, whom she is delighted to see fairly regularly. She keeps up with various local groups and rejoices in the fact that Helmsley, though small, is a vibrant place to live. In addition, Valerie had had a great holiday with **Mary Rusinow (Worthington)** in the Dolomites, Vienna and Salzburg. This year, holiday plans are on hold until her son Simon, who lives in San Francisco, lets the family know about his wedding plans.

Heather Owen (Grange) wrote that last year's long hot summer compensated for long wet winters, past and present, but, unusually for Cornwall, there was a whiteout the week before she sent in her news, with travellers stranded at the Jamaica Inn (an appropriate place for dramatic events, a la Daphne du Maurier!) Heather says she is not keen on being an octogenarian, but fortunately there are quite a few around, and she says she is encouraged by the example of others in the Section. She was looking forward to going to Italy in May with **Bridget Frost (Kell)** and **Caroline Fuchs (Kell)**, on a short tour to Ravenna, and also on her annual visit to Menorca to her daughter's house there. She says that it is a beautiful green island, unspoilt by development. Heather also enjoys occasional trips to London, often to literary lunches organised by *The Oldie* magazine. These are erudite and fun, with famous speakers and camaraderie; she hopes to see some 'old' WB's there some time! Heather concludes by sending "All good wishes to the WB Association, and, of course, the School".

Alison Robinson (de Courcy-Ireland) is still kept busy with family (thirteen grandchildren, six of them now in their twenties!), village affairs, book groups and a weekly shift at the Samaritans, but also managed a cruise on the rivers and canals between St Petersburg and Moscow – fascinating and well worth the hassle of obtaining a Russian visa (sixty-four questions including details of all my children's passport numbers etc!) We followed that earlier this year with a visit to my daughter and her family in Australia, travelling down from Darwin to Adelaide on the famous Ghan train – three luxurious and fascinating days!

Mary Rusinow (Worthington) had had a quieter year. She went back to Italy in April but returned to New York at the end of May for granddaughter's graduation in the General Assembly, with the Secretary General as the main speaker. Granddaughter Ayesha had to present the U Thant prize to this year's recipient, so got to speak. She is now up at Balliol. Mary, having always been forbidden to go to Albania, took a trip down the Dalmatian coast and at least set foot in the country, before returning to Lengstein where Ayesha and a school friend were recovering from their graduation trip round Europe. As Mary says, a bit different from our day! Her trip with **Valerie Moorby** was referred to above. Mary's year was rounded off by Christmas in Pretoria where her son-in-law Sanjay is now UNICEF representative.

Gillian Sandeman (Wright) says she needs no reminders about what old 'Old Girls' we now are - 'the reminders are all around! I'm writing this on Sandy's eighty-sixth birthday; we recently organised a surprise sixtieth birthday party for Deborah and next week I'm flying to England to surprise sister **Jennifer Pellow (Wright)** at **her** eightieth birthday party. How did this happen? And how fortunate we are to be in good health and relatively sound of mind at this stage of our lives.'

Gillian and Sandy were still in Scotland when she wrote last year. They enjoyed a cruise to the Baltics and St Petersburg in May followed almost immediately in early June by their third holiday with a small group of friends, all younger than them, in Macedonia and Greece. Among other wonderful sights, they saw vultures feeding at dawn, the smallest owl in Europe on its nest with babies, and carpets of orchids high up in the Falakro Mountains. They are looking forward to travelling with the group again this July to the Pantanal area of Brazil and Gillian hopes to survive to report on the trip next year!

They went home in June after 10 months away and settled back into life in small town Ontario, finding themselves in one of the hottest summers ever, followed by a really cold winter. Gillian said it is good to be with their Canadian family and friends, but she does miss Edinburgh. 'Life is pretty quiet here: yoga and walking are the limits of my exercise. I'm still on a couple of committees – the Board of our Library and the Board of a halfway house for men coming out of federal prisons – but am not nearly as busy as before we went to Scotland. More time for reading, a lifelong pleasure. And for attacking the big jigsaw on the dining room table. I'm looking forward to the month-long visit by our younger great-granddaughter in May; she'll be three by then, so I expect life to become less quiet and more active for a while!'

Section 23 (1953)
Section Representative:
Jean Stone (Borritt)

Moira Gilbert My grandchildren are growing up too quickly, they are fifteen and nearly twelve now. My younger daughter Dellah's husband is a Commander in the Royal Navy and was in command of a frigate on a seven-month tour which included visits to Australia, New Zealand and Japan. Dellah and daughter Olivia visited him in Japan and Malta.

Caroline Fuchs (Kell) It is three years since my husband died and I am still living (alone) in our big house in North Oxford but, although alone, I am not lonely. Oxford has a great deal to offer and everything is easily accessible. I am in loose contact with **Sally Boston** (in the USA), **Judita Rosenzweig** and **Meg Richardson**. My last visit to Westonbirt was to see a Bampton Opera performance in the lecture hall with picnics in the garden on a perfect summer's day. I was reminded of how beautiful Westonbirt is, something I feel we did not appreciate during our school days. My two daughters and four grandchildren are all doing well, the latter now reaching university age.

Elizabeth Noyce (Clarke) Another year has passed with remarkable speed! Deterioration in health, mainly osteoarthritis, has regretfully interfered with my independence, though fortunately I am still able to drive. 'Wheelie' and walking stick help to keep me reasonably mobile and prevent falls

Family have grown up fast! Richard's Natalie, now twenty-five, has embarked on another degree course; she aims to be a physiotherapist and is now at Cardiff. After gaining a degree at Southampton she spent two years working in a Michelin-star hotel in the summer and looking after chalets in the Alps during the winters. In winter 2017/2018 she and her boyfriend were awarded top of all chalet carers for the whole of Ski World! Her brother, Matthew, the computer wizard, is at present working in Rugby (which he doesn't like!)

Carolyn's family are also doing well. Alex, now twenty-three, is half way towards being fully qualified as a chartered accountant after gaining First Class Honours at Birmingham.

Victoria, now twenty, took a year out after A Levels. She worked in Boots the Chemist for six months and then she and her boyfriend 'did' South East Asia. They toured Thailand, Laos, Cambodia and Vietnam finishing up in Bali, where they did a deep-sea diving course and gained an international certificate.

Following that they inter-railed round European cities for a month! She is now at Nottingham doing graphic design and fashion. She and her course members spent the first week of their second term in New York. Life is very different (and more expensive) these days!

I still belong to the U3A and WI. Days out and different interest sections bring quite a lot of pleasure. We did not go abroad on holiday last year. Terminal 3 airport problems the previous year rather put us off! We still made our trips to Cornwall, but the long drive down there has sadly become more difficult, and we are probably going to have to give it a miss for the time being. We have, however, just booked a week's cruise to Norway in September. We have never cruised before, so this is very much a trial run. Main advantage is that we get picked up from home and brought back again; no driving long distances! I hope to be able to attend the WBA meeting in May and to meet with old friends.

Section 21 & 22 (1951 & 1952)
Section Representative:
Margot Gill (Wilcox)

Elizabeth Daly had a glorious sunny week staying in Hampstead in a house overlooking one of the ponds. She was with one of the families whose children she had 'nannied'. They had a great gathering including Phil, visiting from Birmingham. She went to Kenwood, Golders Hill Park and watched young children in the Lido. She had a trip to Salcombe for a week with family and friends. This year she hopes to return to Ireland where she lived in her early childhood. **Kristen Krabbe (Birchenough)** is her only Westonbirt contact. She says she has lovely friends and enjoys what she can.

Glayne Greenaway (Rocyn Jones) Sadly her husband died after a short illness in March 2018 (our condolences, Glayne). Her family in Paris and New Zealand have been so good and visited a lot and this has helped. She has amazing friends as well. She has had the sad news that **Carol Pompe (Sich)** died after a stroke this February

Lady Henniker (Julia Mason) had a stroke two and a half years ago and lost the use of her left side. She is now in a wheelchair and is planning to move into a home.

Sue Loughnan (Huskisson) is still with us.

Jane Palmer (Needham) says she is fortunate to be still living in part of the converted farmyard of the Manor Farm stables after sixty years. They are thankful to be surrounded by lovely farmland, trees, steams, fantastic wild birds, including a resident skylark, lots of waterfowl on the lake and a plethora of mammals.

At present she is helping write about her district from family farms to the big Caterpillar factory on the old Desford aerodrome site. Many brave young pilots learnt to fly there using double or single wing trainers (tiger moths).

Jane is still a supporter of Leicester City football club – her family have been very involved since 1919. More sad connections with the passing of the legend and charming player, Gordon Banks. He and her father used to meet for lunches when both had retired. He was a most kind man. So, she now has to watch the matches on TV.

Ann Parsons (Leighton) has had a bad year as she broke her femur last June (2018) and has been patched up with metal rods and screws but is still in quite a bit of pain. 'They' think she should have a new hip but apparently it would be a rather traumatic operation with all the metal having to be removed. Horrid decision to make and as usual the consultant refuses to make the decision. 'What a bore it is growing old! I was pretty fit before.'

Jonquil Solt (Denham Davies) She and Bobby are both well and very busy! She is still doing some judging of dressage.

Jenifer Springett says, 'Nothing new' (but at least we know she is still with us. M).

Jane Sutton Another year and she is still grateful to say she is active. She appreciates that she has lost most of her committee work but is grateful to be still continuing to take services in local Anglican and Methodist churches; it gets her out into the country, and she meets such a variety of folk.

The main joy has been getting to know a gifted Kurdish family, refugees from Syria, who are housed in Newbury. The father is a talented sculptor and it has been possible to get him a job with the only company around Newbury that makes sculptures, window frames and mantelpieces. He has fitted in so well. His wife is a real housewife with four delightful children. She has been privileged to be invited to six birthday parties and they have even given one for Jane.

Travelling continues to be on the agenda, to places that have included Norway, Murmansk, the Camargue and a return visit to cousins in Florida.

Margot Gill (Wilcox) Many thanks to those who wrote a reply, much appreciated. The year has been rather hectic as there were three lecture courses – Music, English Language and Pre-History; all very interesting. Had a trip up the A1 to Stamford to see my Shell colleague, on to Bridge of Allan to see step-aunt, then down the M6/5 for a week in Worcester. Luckily, I can take my Peke with me and she does enjoy the car. Norway in the green in summer was a lovely cruise, and the annual trip to Denver was good for relaxation. Are you surprised, as I am, to be around?

Section 19 and 20 (1949-50)
Section Representative:
Serena Jones

Sarah Abel (Poynor) One of the highlights of the year was Westonbirt's ninetieth birthday party, which I attended with my son and his wife. It was very nostalgic to drive in to Piccadilly, to picnic on the lawns, walk round the extensive gardens and into the Italian garden and the golf course, and to go into the church and the converted stables and to tour round the house. All deeply imprinted in my memory and little has changed apart from the closure of Holford House. It was lovely to see the wonderful library restored to its former glory.

Life goes on much the same as usual, except at a slower pace. Last Easter, accompanied by another of my sons, and his wife, I had a happy holiday in Detmold, Germany, and a few days in Devon in the summer. I went to Nottingham and London for Christmas. I have had frequent visits from all my family.

I go to a 'Move to Improve' class twice a week, an Art for Memory Course, and am learning to play jazz piano on an online course.

Janet Brooke (Hutchinson) I have just returned from my annual visit to India where I winter every year. Now an ancient 'Old Girl', I keep going and managed two visits to the school last year accompanied by my daughter who lives nearby. Nothing much has changed, and I felt again the warmth and friendship which enveloped me during the five years that I spent there just after the war. I even managed to sit on my own chair during a service held in Westonbirt Church to celebrate the ninetieth birthday celebrations. Happy memories!

Christine Geach (Wilson) I'm still alive at eighty-nine, but more or less housebound after so many physical mishaps. I seem to visit the hospital nearly every fortnight. Eyesight is pretty bad but at least I can make out what not to fall over! Fizzing in my ears to spoil music. **Joanna** and **Priscilla** died 2 years ago.

Sallie Hotchkin (Bloomer) Has been in contact to confirm her contact details are unchanged.

Dorothy Penny (Robertson) Says she still has her sister, **Elizabeth Hosegood (Robertson)**, living in the north west and who has just turned ninety. Dorothy also remembers **Sarah Abel (Poynor)** whom she used to partner in tennis, and several people in other sections. She downsized home locally last year and is trying to get used to being old!

Meriel Pickett (Sharpe) Following Ben's death, I spent most of the spring in Hungary with my daughter-in-law and their three children. I am useless in the summer there and came home at the end of April to equally debilitating (to me) heat – so the garden grew totally out of hand. I have had a very happy winter pruning back hard, and it is beginning to repay the effort! I am so lucky to have two sons and their families living across the field. I see a great deal of my granddaughters and tiny great-grandson. He is a jolly, happy little boy, who has helped us all. For the first time, I spent Christmas in Varsad, in the snow. Stewed catfish for dinner on Christmas Eve! That was a new experience.

Isla Shewell-Cooper (Fenwick) Has confirmed her email address is unchanged.

Beryl Thorp (Holm) The years continue to pass so quickly and one by one we lose our friends but as my ninety-six-year-old friend says, we must be positive! I had my cataracts 'done' last year and, as everyone says, one's sight improves so much. I do not drive long distances these days but do appreciate having a car.

I continue with my U3A interests which include music and hand bells. I also ring tower bells and our band joined all the churches in the country to ring on 11th November 2018 (one hundred years after WW1). I also enjoy the theatre and concerts when I can. Recently, I had a lovely cruise to the Canaries and went to an opera in the new opera house in Lanzarote. Previously I had done a lot of river cruising. I enjoyed the sun in January.

Elisabeth Wells (Burt) Many thanks to Elisabeth, who sent me her news twice. The first lot never arrived and, when I sent her a reminder, she kindly wrote out some more news: "The bad weather in early March prevented me from going to my brother-in-law's funeral, also Alona, whose flight was cancelled from Berlin. Last June Thames Water discovered a leak in my water supply. They repaired it, sending very competent workmen and put in a stop cock, all for free. I had a lovely week in Ireland at the end of November, terrible weather, staying in Co Clare and then Dublin for granddaughter Holly's graduation from Trinity College, a very impressive and happy day, she was awarded a First."

Elizabeth Wicks (Butcher) I always enjoy the Westonbirt News and realise with much amusement that many years ago in 1948 Section 19 was at the youngsters' end. Now aged eight-seven we oldies are at the back! I am still alive but have sadly been to too many funerals, the saddest being three close members of the family, in particular my dear brother. What a glorious summer we had, I loved it although I believe it was too hot for some. I am still in touch with **Anne Renard** who fell and suffered a fractured femur - such rotten luck. I still drive and feel so lucky to still enjoy that great freedom. I am also very lucky to have two lovely caring daughters. One lives in London and the other in Somerset. Visits to the Big Screen are opportunities to enjoy the ROH, Bolshoi Ballet, Stratford etc.

Sections 17 and 18 (1947-48)
Section Representative:
Pauline Jackson (Garrett)

Primrose Minney writes: 'I loved reading recently in the Newsletter about the restoration work and tried to remember and visualise each room. My family gave me a lovely ninetieth birthday party last August, and I have had cataracts removed since. I have no allergies and am surprisingly free of any medical needs. I live quietly here and enjoy gardening in fine weather. All good wishes to Old Girls, and of course, the school.'

Jean Edwards (Wates) The highlight of last year for Jean was a visit to Rome. Her youngest grandchild is at Worth and he sings in the choir. They were invited to sing Mass in St Peter's and in two other churches. They also sang the Allegri Miserere in the Sistine Chapel, with the high notes sung by girls. She believes that was the first time that this had happened. It was a wonderful experience for them and their families. Her eight other grandchildren all have interesting jobs, varying from doctor, asset manager, and chartered accountant to ISO marketing and sous chef in a pop-up restaurant. Jean states that career opportunities are very different to those in her day.

Hilary Nicholson (Bishop) Hilary has four grandchildren and she tries to keep up with all their world travelling!

Susan Curtis-Bennett Susan is fast approaching her ninetieth birthday on 23rd June. Her family are planning a party for her!

Jennifer Barton Jennifer says she is still keeping going after another variedly busy year although she is finding it much slower getting on with tackling things.

Section 16 (1946)
Section Representative:
Jane Reid

Acknowledgement of the 2018 Summer Newsletter and 2019 AGM notice were received from **Patricia Krichauff (Faulkner)** and **Elizabeth Watson (Allen).**

Ann Ratcliffe (Forsell) died 9 February 2019. Her section representative was informed by her son. He said that Ann always spoke fondly of her time at Westonbirt, not least as one of those that were evacuated to Bowood during World War II. She particularly enjoyed all the sport she did as well as making so many good friends. Her son was sure that Ann would have wished him to thank the Association for sending all the newsletters over the years, which she had really enjoyed reading.

Elizabeth Watson (Allen) sent apologies for the 2019 AGM.

Section 15 (1945)
Section Representative:
Serena Jones

June Fulford (Layborn) I am still in touch with **Liz Hosegood (Robertson)** but afraid all my other Westonbirt contacts are gone. Family interests keep me busy; I now have two great granddaughters and two great grandsons, which is lovely. Life, even nearing 91, is good and I've been very lucky. I still remember Miss Grubb's words: 'You earn rights, you inherit duties'. What a pity that isn't true today (don't I sound like a cranky old lady!).

Mercia MacDermott In all probability, by the time you read this, I shall be ninety-two, but am lucky to be still pretty mobile, and I walked about three miles during a recent visit to Kew Gardens. I am still President of the Friends of Worthing Museum, though my duties are not very onerous, and consist mainly in giving the vote of thanks after our monthly lectures.

Lone Red Poppy, a biography of the Bulgarian Socialist leader, Dimiter Blagoer, which I wrote quite a long time ago, appeared in a Bulgarian translation in 2018, and received several awards in Bulgaria. 'For Freedon and Perfection', the biography of the Bulgarian national hero, Yane Sandansky, which I wrote many years ago, is due to appear in a French translation in France this year. I am no longer writing books, and am enjoying reading other people's books, especially ones about geology and evolution.

Sections 13-14 (1943-44)
Section Representative:
Serena Jones

After sixty-five years as Section Rep, Jean Marr recently asked if someone could please take over these sections, and I volunteered. Jean became Section Rep in 1953, and in 2015 she was given Honorary Membership of the Association in recognition of her amazingly long service (you could argue it was well overdue!) Thank you so much, Jean, for doing a grand job over so many years.

Sadly, my first job is to record the deaths of **Patricia Hall (Dickinson)** and **Sue Yealland (Simpson)** who both died last summer.

Felicity Atkinson (Sutton) I had a phone call from Felicity's son who told me that Felicity now has dementia and doesn't remember very much. He asked for her to be taken off the mailing list, which I have done.

Gillian Blum (Gregory) In February I celebrated my ninety-third birthday and had a lovely family get together. I became a great-grandparent for the fourth time just before Christmas. Now I am waiting to have a new heart valve as I have aortic stenosis.

Rosemary Campbell (Fraser) The two friends I kept in touch with have both died: **Elizabeth Lambton** and **Elizabeth Burnett (Clark-Turner)**. The trouble is that contemporaries are so old – I look at the *Daily Telegraph* every day to keep in touch.

Unfortunately, I broke a leg about four years ago and now have to walk with a frame. I gave up driving as it was impossible to continue, sadly. I lived at Wasing Lodge, about two miles from here, for over sixty years and loved it, but it was a little dangerous going out onto the main road and too large for me. So, I live in my daughter's house, which is better, and I have a stairlift (very necessary). My mind is fine, which is wonderful.

My second son, James who is a clergyman is East Sussex, married a Westonbirt girl, **Mary Campbell (Rolston)** who will be sixty-one in May. *(Yes, I remember Mary. She and her sister, Alicia, were both in Badminton. One was a year older and one a year younger than me. SJ)*

Mary Capey (Reynolds) The sale of my house has taken over two years – infuriating but now just legally complete. Stonegate, where I am now, is a lovely estate encircled by trees and blossom. All maintenance of the flat's exterior and the garden are done by the management. I have a long sitting room with windows on all sides except north, but I spend hours trying to cook on a small electric cooker and microwave after being used to an Aga all my married life.

I am definitely feeling old age creeping up. I still sing in the church choir but have given up the choral society as I cannot stand long enough for concerts. I have given away my car – can't face the traffic – and I go about in an electric buggy (with a fair turn of speed). My back and legs are not much use.

Jean Marr Jean phoned me with her news and said she has been through the mill health-wise recently, due to a very swollen right leg, which the doctors had problems diagnosing. She was in hospital for several weeks and dosed up with so much medication she can't remember much about it, nor about Christmas. Thankfully she is better now, and we had a lovely chat. She told me that she always wears her Amaryllis brooch.

She mentioned that she was bridesmaid to **Gwyneth Hadcock** (one of the three Hadcock sisters) and is also godmother to Gwyneth's daughter, who lives up in Scotland. It's a far cry from Devon, but Jean reckons she will one day move to Scotland.

I see **Elizabeth Wicks** and **Jenny Dean** from time to time. I don't go to local societies (WI, historical, gardening etc.) because I don't stay awake after about 9pm! I have eight grandchildren and to date nine great-grandchildren, now very near and they all visit, or I visit them if collected.

Sections 1-12 (1931-42)
Serena Jones (Sections 1-8), Pauline Jackson (Section 9), Rebecca Williams (Sections 10-12)

There are no active members in Sections 1–8, and no news from Sections 9–12.

Invitation to Westonbirt Association Members

Westonbirt School always welcomes alumnae, whether on formal occasions such as Association Days, or for informal visits to reminisce about your school days. There's always something new to see, in terms of academic and extra-curricular activities, new buildings and projects to restore the old, and current pupils are always fascinated to meet their predecessors. You are also very welcome to bring your family, even if you have no daughters or granddaughters to follow in your academic footsteps!

In the interests of security, and to make sure we are able to welcome you on your preferred date, please contact **Mrs Rhiannon Roche, PA to the Headmistress, to arrange your visit by calling 01666 880333 or emailing rroche@westonbirt.gloucs.sch.uk.**

Whether or not you plan to visit the school in person, you may also like to visit our website, which is constantly being updated with school news and photos, as well as a picture gallery from the archives.

How to Contact the Westonbirt Association

The Westonbirt Association database is kindly managed by the School, and so the School is now your first point of contact for any enquiries regarding the Association. **Mrs Rhiannon Roche, PA to the Headmistress**, will be able to direct you to the most appropriate person, according to the nature of your query. She will also be able to provide contact details for your Section Representative, whose personal information is no longer included in the News Magazine for the sake of their privacy.

Incidentally, please don't forget to let **Rhiannon k**now if your own contact details change, so that we can keep you informed of Association matters and can find you if any of your former classmates are looking for you. If you're a fan of social media, you may also enjoy networking with us on the alumni Facebook page:

www.facebook.com/groups/108986984329/

Rhiannon works at the school full time, year-round, so is generally available during office hours. You may reach her via the main school telephone number, 01666 880333, or by emailing her at rroche@westonbirt.gloucs.sch.uk. She is always glad to hear from past pupils.

How to Order Copies
of the Westonbirt Association News

Since 2015, to gain efficiencies, save costs, and to take advantage of advances in modern technology, we have changed the way we produce and distribute the Westonbirt Association News.

If you are a regular subscriber, you are welcome to go on receiving your copy as before, despatched by the News Finances and Distribution Officer, Jenny Webb, for as long as your account with her is in sufficient credit.

However, you will also now be able to order the latest edition, and all future editions, online, wherever you live in the world. Your copy will be printed in your local territory and sent at local postage rate. If you do this while your account with Jenny is still in credit, she will refund the balance on request - or if you prefer, you may simply donate the balance to the Westonbirt Association Memorial Bursary Fund.

If you prefer not to order online, you may also be able to order a print copy from your local high street bookshop by providing them with the ISBN number of the latest edition.

If, on the other hand, you are one of the many people who prefer these days to read ebooks, you may prefer to order an ebook version, which will be made available via all the mainstream ebook platforms, including Kindle, Kobo and iBooks.

We are confident that this is the best way forward for the long-term interests of the Association, and we hope it will also appeal to the younger generation (and many of the older ones!) who enjoy using digital technology. Please be assured, however, that we will always produce print copies for those who prefer them, and also for our substantial Association News archive.

Westonbirt Association
Memorial Bursary Fund

The Westonbirt Association Memorial Bursary was set up in the late 1940s in memory of the five former Westonbirt pupils who lost their lives during the Second World War while they were members of the Forces, Civil Defence or the Nursing Services.

The aim of the fund is to give a bursary each year to help fund the school fees of girls at the school. The Memorial Bursary is still running today, and each year the Association makes an award from this fund to help towards the sixth form fees of one or more pupils.

To be considered for the Memorial Bursary, girls must be nominated by the school in the spring of their Year 11. Candidates complete an application form and are interviewed by a panel from the Westonbirt Association Committee. The process provides good experience for later job and university applications, and, for the successful candidate, receipt of the award enhances their CV as well as providing welcome financial help. Once awarded, payment is made for both years of the recipient's sixth form.

Over the years, we have helped more than eighty pupils in this way. With income levels from investments so low at present, and school fees rising, new donations are always welcome to increase the value of the award.

How to Donate to the Memorial Bursary Fund

Cash donations

Payments may be made by cheque payable to "Westonbirt School" and should be clearly marked for the Westonbirt Association Memorial Bursary Fund.

Online by standing order

Please reference payment in the following format:

>Account name: Westonbirt School
>Sort code: 200384
>Account number: 30951927
>Bank: Barclays

Bequests

As the school is a charity, bequests are free from liability to inheritance tax. The following are suitable words to send to your solicitor with a request that the Westonbirt Association Memorial Bursary be included in your will:

>*"I bequeath to Westonbirt School in the county of Gloucestershire the sum of £x, free of duty, to be used for the purposes of the Westonbirt Association Memorial Bursary."*

You might also wish to inform the school as follows:

>*"I intend to make a bequest to the school for the purposes of the Westonbirt Association Memorial Bursary."*

GiftAid Declaration for the Westonbirt Association Memorial Bursary

If you are a UK taxpayer, the school can reclaim tax on any gifts you make, via the Gift Aid scheme, provided you fill in the declaration form below in full and return it with your first gift.

Please treat as Gift Aid donations all qualifying gifts of money made *(please circle as applicable)*: *today / in the past 4 years / in the future*

I enclose a donation of £.......... as a contribution to the Westonbirt Association Memorial Bursary.

I confirm I have paid or will pay an amount of income tax or capital gains tax for each tax year (6 April to 5 April) that is at least equal to the amount of tax that Westonbirt School and all other charities that I donate to will reclaim on my gifts for that tax year. I understand that other taxes such as VAT and council tax do not qualify. I understand the charity will reclaim 25p on every £1 that I give on or after 6 April 2008.

Title_____ Forename _____

Surname_____

Address_____

Postcode_____

Signature_____

Date_____

Please notify Westonbirt School if you want to cancel this declaration OR change your name or home address OR no longer pay sufficient tax on your income and/or capital gains. If you pay income tax at the higher or additional tax rate and want to receive the additional tax relief due to you, you must include all your Gift Aid donations on your self-assessment tax return.

Please send donations and the completed form to:
The Finance Manager, The Bursary, Westonbirt School
Tetbury, Gloucestershire GL8 8QG
Registered Charity Number 311715

*We would like to thank Alanbrookes Ltd
for kindly auditing the Association's accounts.*

ALANBROOKES LTD
CHARTERED ACCCOUNTAND AND REGISTERED AUDITOR

We aim to bring transformational change to local businesses
and the lives of their owners.
Please call Andrew Fisher for a free exploratory meeting
on 01453 889559 or email andrewfisher@alanbrookes.co.uk
www.alanbrookes.co.uk

www.ingramcontent.com/pod-product-compliance
Lightning Source LLC
Chambersburg PA
CBHW071349080526
44587CB00017B/3029